Preparation and Renovation

Building **You** and **Marriage** Relationships on the **"Rock"**

CLIFTON L. POWELL

Contact us:
powellrelationshipministries@gmail.com
P.O. Box 271 Butner N.C. 27509

ISBN: 9798324686413

Table of Contents

Foreword

Greetings! Pastor Clifton L. Powell,

I am thrilled and deeply moved by your decision to write this book on relationships and marriages. As I reflect on the day we first met, I vividly remember feeling the presence of the Holy Spirit coming out of you. Your unwavering love for Christ shines through the anointing that's on your life and it has been such an inspiration to others.

Your dedication and support for AWMTT's day-to-day prayer line have not gone unnoticed. Your participation has been a source of strength and encouragement for so many of us. Your commitment to guiding others in their spiritual journey is truly commendable, and I am grateful for the impact you've had on our ministry.

I have no doubt that your book will be a beacon of hope and wisdom for countless individuals seeking guidance in their relationships. Your insights, rooted in scripture and enriched by your faith, will undoubtedly touch the hearts and minds of so many people.

Thank you for your steadfast commitment to spreading the love of Christ and for your desire to share your perception and knowledge through this book. May God continue to bless you abundantly as you embark on this new chapter of your ministry.

With heartfelt gratitude,

Dr. Vivian Geter

Introduction

Matthew 19:6 What therefore God hath joined together let not man put asunder.

It is always God's will that married couples stay together. Again, the scripture says that which God puts together let no man put asunder. Unfortunately, some marriages were not put together by God, while others came together but were not prepared for the days ahead. Make no mistake about it, it's always in the Father's will that we live happy lives. Many have testified that they were happier when they were single. Others were honest enough to say that they witnessed in their spirit on their wedding day not to marry the individual before them. Parents and guardians were in disagreement with the union but remained silent, wishing later that they should have agreed with their parental instincts about what they felt was in the best interest for their son or daughter. I pray that the tools in this book will provide an avenue to help lower the divorce rate. Approximately 40-50% of first marriages end in divorce. The rate for second marriages is even higher, 60-67%. One of the reasons I believe the rates are so high is due to the lack of preparation. One of the contributing factors to a lack of preparation for marriages is not having the sufficient amount of knowledge that is required. Hosea 4:6 My people are destroyed for a lack of knowledge. Many couples get married but circumstances and challenges that arise prove that they were not as ready as they believed they were.

Jeremiah 23:18 For who hath stood in the counsel of the Lord, and perceived and heard his Word? As I face the challenge of seeking the face of the Lord for answers for His people, I can honestly say that I was blessed with the wealth of knowledge that the Father loosed into my spirit to give to His people. I refer to the Lord sometimes by calling Him a solution-oriented God. Matthew 9:36 But when He (Jesus) saw the multitude, He was moved with compassion because they fainted and were scattered abroad… In the midst of people giving up, caving in, even quitting on having a desire to get married or married again, my prayer is that you receive the compassion that is in my heart for marriages as well as the insights that are revealed in this book in hopes that it could rekindle a desire in your heart for that which God calls honorable (Hebrews 13:4). **Marriage is honorable.** The uprooting of pain and the repairing of trust are two essential ingredients that are needed to renovate your marriage. God promises to restore the unhealthy years of marriage that were lost. (Joel 2:25) But let us be real, it's a process. So allow the wisdom, knowledge and understanding that is contained in this book begin to launch you toward renovating your marriage to shine to the glory of God.

Also to the singles who desire to be married, examine the marriages that you see around you. Don't be judgmental or critical. Learn from the mistakes that we've made and purpose with all of your heart not to repeat them as you prepare for your husband or wife. Remember the words of wisdom of the late Dr. Myles Munroe saying, "Wisdom is not power, but *applied* wisdom is power." So as you are preparing for your mate in the future, which I am hoping for you would be God's good, acceptable, and perfect will, with no sorrows added, take inventory of the things that you've been through, any hurts, any pains, any wrong marriages that were modeled before you, to make the necessary corrections before you proceed in connecting with someone. (Psalms 147:3) He heals the broken-hearted… Lastly, my encouragement to you is to get healed from previous relationships or any pain that you experienced in your upbringing. This will allow you to connect with someone else in a new relationship being healthy and avoiding the pain of the past.

Father, in the name of Jesus, I pray that the contents in this book will help all of our marriages to make the necessary upgrades. A husband or wife who reads this book will no longer have to just tolerate the person that they're married to, but with the tools that are given here, they can begin to celebrate one another. And Lord for the singles, my prayer is that they have a blessed, healthy marriage of not just happiness but joy and peace as they pursue the person that You've blessed them with to be an asset to their lives and not a liability, and that they refuse to compromise their standards in their pursuit of marriage. And also, God let Your grace be released upon any individual that reads this book and does not desire to get married yet or again. May they know that it's OK to glorify You in their body, their spirit and their soul while giving themselves wholly to You. May the joy of the Lord continue to be their strength.

In Jesus' name,

Amen.

Acknowledgements

To my grandmothers, the late Izolia Holloway and the late Sarah P. Grant: You were such spiritual pillars to me in my upbringing. Also to my late mother, Mary Sandra Powell Lipscomb: I thank you for taking me to the house of God to be trained up in the way that I should go, when there was so much temptation in our community that could have derailed God's purpose for my life. (Reggie and Terry, We made it!)

To the men of God that sowed the Word of God into my spirit: the late Bishop A. W. Lawson, the late Pastor Rupert L. Dudley, and Bishop Elroy Lewis: Thank you for imparting the wisdom of God that helped to form a solid foundation and relationship with Jesus Christ.

To Apostle Donald Q. Fozard: Truly you are a general in the kingdom of God. Many pastors followed the pattern you set. Thank you for licensing me and ordaining me in the ministry.

To Pastor Brenda Timberlake: Thank you for being there, pouring in the oil and the wine during a season of rebuilding in my life as well as that of my family's. Being in the presence of healthy marriages was very beneficial to me and my wife.

To my Now Church family under the leadership of Pastor Nate Davis, Jr. and Lady Tequilla Davis: Thank you guys for leading what I believe to be one of the best congregations for someone that needs a good church family to connect to and experience faith, family, and community in their everyday lives.

To mother Vivian Geter, the staff of AWMTT, and all the ministry gifts associated with such an awesome organization: Thank you for believing in me and trusting in the gift of God that's on my life. You are people of class, good character, and integrity.

To my sister/mother, Minister Anita Williams: Truly the apples don't fall far from the tree. The spirit of counsel that rested on our mother that's now on you, has made its way upon me. I really appreciate you.

To my bonus parents, David A. Best, Sr. and the late Priscilla Robinson Best: Thank you guys for receiving us. We LOVE being a part of your family!

Lastly to the love of my life, Staris Best Powell, and my children Christian, Christina, Caiden, and Cayla: Thank you guys for enduring the process with me. God is causing all things to work together for our good.

The Original Wedding Vow

*There is a difference also between a wife and a virgin. The unmarried woman cares for the things of the Lord that she may be holy, both in body and in spirit, but she that is married cares for the things of the world, how she may please her husband. And this I speak for your own profit, not that I should cast a snare upon you, but for that which is calmly, that **ye may attend unto the Lord without distraction**.*

1 Corinthians 7:34-35

A Significant Distraction

And the Lord emphasized to me, something that He wanted to catch my attention at the end of vs 35, "Ye may attend unto the Lord without distraction." Paul strategically included this as it would have a great significance. What seems to be a minor detail, proves rather to have great impact. There's something that happens in the life of a man as he transitions from being single unto the Lord to choosing a mate. Likewise, there is something that happens in the life of a woman, who is single unto the Lord, when she is chosen as a helpmate.

To say that the single man and the single woman being chosen, forgets the word "distraction", is a stretch. The happy couple has so many other things on their mind, paying little attention to distractions. Besides, if it was so important,

1

wouldn't it have come up during marriage counseling? How relevant can it be? The truth is, when you choose to be married, life as you know it will change.

Your life is going to be distracted. Distractions can prevent someone from giving their full attention to something else. Distractions are extreme agitations of the mind and emotions. Distractions can cause an individual to turn their attention away from something they prefer to concentrate on, to something that matters to another. Ready or not, distractions are going to come. No one is exempt! You are soon to be affected by your mate's, likes and dislikes. These serve as distractions even for those already married and even for those who have championed this thing called marriage.

Significant Grace

Children from a previous relationship can serve as a distraction. A ready-made family requires sacrifice. The person connecting with a parent with children, should be father or mother material. When God joins together a man and a woman, He gives them individually grace to deal with the distractions that will come. The same grace that connects you is extended to one another in the form of special attention, consideration, and support when needed.

When God joins two people together, they start out with a healthy advantage. Part of that advantage is the confidence that come with knowing that God approves, from the get-go.

Celebrity (Novelty), Vows

It's new, its hip, it's unusual, and it's marketable. Who knew that there would come a time when couples would side with your favorite celebrity's vow. Couples seemingly want to do something different, something exotic, like patterning their vows after a TV personality. Let's do it like they did it! Let's write our own vows.

The booby trap of writing their own vows was that they did not stop to understand the substance that's in what I call the ***"original wedding vow"***.

3

There is substance in there to be considered, before you even say, I do.

The original wedding vows consist of:

- To HAVE and to hold
- For BETTER or worse
- For RICHER or poorer
- In SICKNESS and in health
- To LOVE and to cherish
- Until DEATH do us part

This listing of the wedding vow alone could make up a counseling session.

To HAVE and to Hold

To hold is to be committed! To be committed includes being affectionate and tenderhearted to each other. Commitment involves physical, mental, emotional, and spiritual support for one another. To have, is to receive without any reservation. Couples would do well to stop and examine any reservations, uneasiness, or hesitations. Are there any red flags? Has anyone approached you with claims of having discernment or perception of your future mate? Has your engagement been extended? How often do you change your wedding date? All these things and more contribute to reservations.

I would be remised if I didn't mention if the groom felt uneasy when putting the ring on his brides' finger. Some guys I know confessed to an uneasiness, a check in their spirit before the bride to be, walked down the aisle. These were more than misgivings, jitters, or anxiety. The Holy Spirit was trying to get their attention. They later replied: "I did it anyway."

...And it is the Spirit that beareth witness, because the Spirit is truth.

I John 5:6b

To have and to hold means to receive without reservation, the total gift of another person. The person God brings to you is a gift. A gift is something or someone that benefits you. A gift is to be an addition and a multiplication. Whenever something or someone subtracts or divides, it causes sorrows in your life, it is not a gift.

To have is not a statement of just partnership. It is rather a promise of unconditional acceptance. All those who desire to do whatever they want to do, whenever they get ready to do it, should stay single. This bears repeating: STAY SINGLE! When you say to have and to hold, this includes your body also. These are preparatory words that set the tone and atmosphere for the married couple's times of physical intimacy. Your body is not your own. This is not said to provoke you to wrath, to quarrel or to debate with you about something God designed to enhance your relationship. Understanding the will and intentions of God is what makes us fruitful in our attitude in every aspect of the marriage relationship.

We are instructed in 1 Corinthians 7:2 - "Nevertheless, to avoid fornication, let every man have his own wife and let every woman have her own husband." To have means to receive without reservation, without being cautious, on-guard or have constant suspicion. It means that he or she is exclusively yours. Verse 3, further instructs, "Let the husband render unto the wife due benevolence: and likewise, also the wife unto the husband. Marriage involves commitment. Part of that commitment is to give your conjugal physical rights over to your husband, and over to your wife. Verse 4, compliments the proceeding verses saying, "The wife hath not power of her own body, but the husband: and likewise, also the husband hath not power over his own body, but the wife."

Too often we gloss over **"DEFRAUD" YE NOT ONE ANOTHER**, except it be with consent

for a time, that ye may give yourselves to fasting and prayer; and come together again, that Satan tempt you not for your incontinency." If your desire is to stay single, don't get married! If your desire is to be selfish with that which is due to your mate, stay single! Don't get married! For those of you who are already married, listen carefully: God does not approve of the emotional witchcraft you use on your mate. You are not justified when you develop an attitude that suggests that husband or wife has to do something to earn sex with you. The wrong attitude says, you didn't clean up enough, you didn't buy what I deserved, you didn't get me a bigger ring. You withhold from your spouse and manipulate things just to have your way.

Marriage Is for Grown People

You are that man's wife. That's who you are. You are the one he decided to be exclusive with. His open commitment to you conveyed that you added value to him. Don't you think it's about time you acknowledge who you are? When you acknowledge who you are, then your behavior will reflect it. You are NOT a trick. Excuse my language, but you are NOT a call girl. You are NOT for hire. He should never have to work or earn the comforts that are essential to the marriage relationship. You entered into an agreement. You entered a covenant. You entered into a legal binding agreement to supply, to come together with him.

Believe it or not, you are putting your marriage in jeopardy. Don't take the risk of destroying the mental, emotional and physical pillars by choosing not to supply. It is a choice that you make. Like all other choices, this one also comes with consequences. Withholding conjugal rights from your husband only damages your mental intimacy and emotional intimacy. The entire intimacy realm is affected when you work emotional witchcraft on your husband or on your wife.

Come out of the world. That's the way worldly people carry on. Your husband or wife does not have to earn you. You are not a harlot! Men you are not a gigolo. Stop making your spouse pay. Stop making the one you chose, suffer.

That "Satan Tempt You Not"

Both husbands and wives, in and outside of the church are suffering! While some are vocal about their struggle, others are suffering in silence. The Bible is very clear about the warfare encountered by the husband or that wife when they are defrauded. Let's look at I Corinthians 7:5. That passage of scripture begins and ends with a bang: that "Satan tempt you not,". Satan takes any advantage you give him. You are responsible to your own mate to supply. To deny your mate, is to allow your husband or your wife to be tempted in this area that is now lacking because of your unwillingness and or selfishness.

It is important to cover your mate with consistency. Inconsistency can open the door for emotional adultery. This can be a consequence of the burning (yearning, unfulfilled appetite, or natural desire ignored). Now, your spouse is looking at other people in ways that they shouldn't because you are not covering or supplying them of what God ordained to come through you.

Therefore, if you do not want to be able to supply the intimacy due to your mate, don't get married. These are genuine concerns. None of us are trouble exempt. None of us should be confident in the flesh. – Philippians, 3:3

Striving In the Face of Difficulty

Simply put, struggling is striving in the face of difficulty. There are so many reasons why wives and why husbands are accomplices when it comes to their mate's struggle. They have decided to stop supplying the need. Their spouse consequently is in the valley of temptation, engaged in a struggle that without fasting and praying, may open the door for adultery.

It is in fasting and praying that God begins to work on the heart of your spouse so that neither of you enter any entanglements.

And she caught him by his garment, saying, Lie with me: and he left his garment in her hand, and fled, and got him out.

Genesis 39:12

The enemy wants to capitalize on every perceived opportunity. Don't allow him to catch you by your garment. Be careful how you hear. Don't allow yourself to be in close quarters with them.

A Carefully Devised Plan

His master's wife cast her eyes upon Joseph – Genesis 39:7

But he refused – Genesis 39:8

How can I do this great wickedness, and sin against God? – Genesis 39:9

She spoke to Joseph, day by day – Genesis 39:10

There was none of the men of the house there within – Genesis 39:11

You may have a co-worker taking notice. You may have somebody that's watching you, eyeing you down, watching you like a hawk. They have convinced themselves that their designs on you will work. The follow up is to drop some seeds that could speak to a vulnerable place in you. Sweet words, telling you how handsome or how beautiful you are.

This is where we should take a page out of Joseph's playbook. The compliments kept coming --   A little praise here, a pat on the back there. It wasn't the words alone; it was more about the intention(s) of the one speaking.

Potipher's wife was ambitious. She said what she thought Joseph needed to hear. She spoke to him daily the kinds of words that would intoxicate most men. Her hopes were that eventually he would be delighted to see her coming.

Shall I sin against God? Shall I do this sin against God? Confession is good for the soul. He remembered and confessed his loyalty to God. He was stirred, but not by her words. God had been constant. God was his never-ending, around the clock, steadfast hope. There was enough in him, that did not want to let God down. Joseph stood and overcame her advances, even when they were alone.

Be Consistent in Having and Holding

Commitment without reservation is to have and to hold. It includes the comfort of being able to give yourself exclusively to your spouse. It includes rendering yourself, giving benevolence to your covenant partner. It is important to remember that the original vows have much more substance than the new, hip, seemingly exotic, novelty vows. Their shine shall soon wear off. All relationships come with challenges. One of the significances of saying "I do", is that you continue to operate in grace toward your mate. Defrauding your husband or wife makes you an accomplice to their suffering. Please, don't make them suffer.

For Better or for Worse

Are we really ready for *"NO MATTER WHAT HAPPENS"*? Trying situations are going to come against, our marriage! Individuals must deal with urgent circumstances. From one moment to the next, things can get awkward, and you find yourself frustrated. Situations will counter or set themselves against any good thing that you anticipate happening. …And as rewarding as our children are, the devil can try and use them in some capacity to provoke a "real moment".

Must everything be perfect? NO! Are we intimidated by imperfect moments, NO! However, I'm thinking that the bride to be and the groom to be would like as much as possible to be prepared.

Psalms 34:19 says, "Many are the afflictions of the righteous, but the Lord will deliver them out of them all."

It's a bonus to your relationship to understand how some afflictions TRY and continue or stay alive by ignoring specific patterns in the bloodline of your happy bride or handsome groom. You're not looking for an opening to ghost the person you're committed to. You should consider some fasting and praying and speaking with a counselor, as you may encounter some sensitive areas, that will take more than a discussion and dinner to heal.

You must find out beforehand what's on assignment with your mate's family bloodline. You may be dating somebody that has a closed heart. They may appear on the surface as someone who just isn't emotional. You notice more often that they don't talk much. In attempting to know them better, it's hard to get them to share the secrets of their heart.

One of the things the Holy Spirit says, "Study the others in the person's family." Watch out for a person that has gained your interest who never wants to bring you around his or her family. That's a red flag right there. That may indicate that there is something to hide. Sometimes the patterns in the blood line of the person you are dating are not as obvious until you recognize it in their siblings, in their parents and grandparents.

Marriage is Not for Dummies

Know what you are getting into! You don't want to connect with someone where the warfare is greater than what you can handle. What are some patterns in the blood line? Are there abuses? Is there residue from previous relationships? As your relationship evolves, you need to get information about them, or your hope of matrimony will fizzle out. For better, for worse, should indicate that you have some idea who you are standing with and what you are standing against. I Peter 3:7, says, "Now, husbands dwell with your wife according to knowledge giving honor unto the wife."

Not everyone is a candidate for, for better, for worse! You've got to find out what you are getting into or else you're going to go through all types of things. Don't wait until you've said, "I do". There are many discontented husbands and wives who've met the unexpected, after exchanging these vows. The Apostle Paul says, "For I have learned in whatever state that I'm in to be content." The Holy Spirit had to help him get to this place.

*Not that I speak in respect of want; for I have
learned, in whatsoever state I am, therewith to
be content.*

*I know both how to be abased, and I know how
to be abound: everywhere and in all things I am
instructed both to be full and to be hungry, both
to abound and to suffer need.*

Philippians 4:11-12

Unfortunately, some of you don't have this testimony.
Contentment is different from settling. Contentment
incorporates ease, while settling can include doing things to
smooth over or just dealing with things as they occur. Hats off
to those husbands and wives who have learned what it means
to be content, in whatever state.

The time to get information is now. Set yourself up for
success. For some, it would be rewarding to extend the time of
engagement to better prepare. Microwave engagements have
been attributed to being caught up in the moment. The moment
was right, the mood was perfect. We were already in Belize
vacationing on the beach, It was so tranquil, and the weather
spoke to us. Others bragged about being in Cancun or being in
the Dominican Republic. We were on the island for goodness'
sake. The atmosphere was stunning.

Not long after getting engaged, the dresses were ordered
soon after. The bridesmaids had picked out the colors and in all
the excitement, the real work necessary was being neglected.
Whatever you don't deal with before you get married, is harder
to deal with afterwards.

Take the time to deal with, sort out and attend to matters upfront. Don't shy away from background checks (criminal history, medical history, family history and identity verification). Be ready to tackle the hidden things when they show up. Don't be amongst those who reluctantly say, "I didn't know that. I did not know that about him. I never knew. I wasn't aware of that".

You didn't ask him. You did not find out about her. "I got love on my mind" won't matter when those unimaginable things show up after the vows. I know you meant it when you said for better, for worse …Yet you never thought that it would come to this.

Refuse to connect with a person under the idea of for better or for worse. Without the proper information those worse times will come. Many times, it's unpreparedness that designates it as worse. If only you had time to prepare. If only you knew about the finances. If only you were aware of the sickness.

How Much Should I Tolerate?

The definition of for better or worse does not mean that you allow yourself to be a victim. You are not required to sit back and take the abuse of a cheating spouse. For better or worse does not require you to tolerate his/her committing adultery and still having sex with you. Infidelity in marriage opens the door for sexually transmitted diseases.

I have a problem with St. Luke 16:8, which says, "The children of this world are in this generation wiser than the children of the light." Even those who aren't born again sometimes operate with more discretion that Christians. There are somethings sinner won't even tolerate with that born again, spirit filled Christians condone.

Once the trust is broken and infidelity is committed the partner is forbidden to sleep in the same bed. They give each other ultimatums, either you leave the house or I will. The adultery is met with an attitude of indifference. The response of their spouse is one of offense. The husband or wife perpetrating the adultery is made to feel some remorse for the inexcusable act. Adultery was committed! Get counseling! Before you begin to participate in engagements again, seek counseling.

For better or for worse is not putting up with a spouse's addiction. "Keep quiet while I spoke pot," was not in the wedding vows. Physical abuse by husband or wife, was not a part of the contract. You have to know when to leave the individual and get counseling. Some situations demand that the abuser get help through anger management courses. Don't suffer in silence and allow yourself to get knocked upside the head. Verbal abuse can be just as bad. Verbal abuse in the form of verbal attacks, harassment, or the use of silence as a weapon is not what you signed up for. God is not ordering you to be mishandled as a means of trying your faith. No, God is not using this abuse as a tool for the enemy to try your marriage.

Beloved, don't be driven by your emotions. Refuse to be steered, compelled or urged to do something that is not in your best interest. Don't allow your emotions to drive you to do things impulsively. Dr. Myles Munroe spoke one of the greatest hinderances to spiritual discernment is when your human emotions get in the way. Both men and women with great callings and giftings of discernment have been sifted because of it.

Prophetic warnings have been given. Advance information was imparted. God was specific in what the vessel was to do. God was making a way of escape. The charge was to stay away. …And for a while the urgency of the message saved her life. Everything was well, until the day that she was convinced to let down her guard and return.

This story has happened to so many others who leaned in the moment to their emotions rather than obeying God. How great a fall! What a great cost! A good use of judgement could have saved them a lifetime of sorrow or a loss of life.

Get Out of There!

Once you have identified that it is abuse, get out of there! Recognize when you need help. Avoid the traumas associated with abandonment. When a person decides to leave you and leave the children, you have to set up boundaries. As long as you allow them to occasionally stop by, they will exploit you. Don't allow them to treat you like a sex object. When possible, move out of the house.

There are many people, like some of you, who wrestle with "how much do I take?" You have made "for better or worse" a holding place where you subject to physical abuse, mistreatment, all types of ridicule. For many is it a holding place for their mate to undermine and dominate them.

Despite the audible rejection of how they were being mishandled, they never followed up. They declared that they were no longer going to take it, but the abuser was never convicted. At some point the person being victimized must get some backbone. Stand up for yourself. Give yourself the support you need by remembering that God loves you and that you deserve better. His or her leaving you and the family is abandonment. When your mate is wilding out because of frequent drug usage don't be afraid to admit to yourself first that they have an addiction. You must know when things have escalated to the degree that you need to separate in order for your spouse to get some help.

Your Perspective On It Makes the Difference

Trying times are up ahead! A difficult circumstance, a sorrowful event or some aspect that seems out of your control is coming your way. Now, keep calm!

I know how to be abased and I know how to abound: everywhere and in all things, I am instructed both to be full and to be hungry, both to abound and to suffer need.

Philippians 4:12

Seasons change and people retire. Unexpected health challenges can affect your bank balance. When you go from a two-family income to one, money has to be managed differently. You can, however, survive times of financial adjustments in the house. A most valuable lesson can be learned from St. Luke 12:13-15. It sums up in "...a man's life consisteth not in the abundance of the things which he possesseth".

Your perspective on your situation, makes the difference.

Building bigger barns may not be the answer. (Read vs. 16-21) Jesus gave the illustration of the man that built barns and had bigger barns. And Jesus said "Thy fool, this night, thy soul shall be required of thee. And who shall those things be that you have gathered up to yourself?" So Jesus began to emphasize the difference in having things and not be rich towards God. In a marriage both the husband and his wife need to be rich towards God. Likewise, trying times won't betray the wife. Their spiritual intimacy will in times of financial situations cause them to trust in the Lord instead of becoming panic-stricken. This is a MUCH better scenario than one where the wife and/or husband, leaving and parachuting out of the house because of a financial setback.

Instruct Me in the Way That I Shall Go…

Count up the cost! Jesus says, in St. Luke 14:28, "For which of you sitting attending to build a tower should have not down first counteth (calculated) the cost." Please, stop a moment and meditate on His words.

Many people have this testimony, that they depended on money to answer for it all (Ecclesiastes 10:19). Vows and loans, contracts and purchases are made with having a sufficient amount of money to handle our wants. Times of plenty can be blinding and couples forget to prepare for "rainy days". They don't anticipate a time when situations might be tight and fail to budget for it. They didn't count up the cost.

For richer or for poorer requires that you adjust your budget or start a budget if there is not one. Shame is the enemy of getting started. Husbands must come together with their wives. This is not the time for self-preservation. You've got to begin to come together to reason. Don't allow who makes the most or the least money derail what you are trying to accomplish together.

What's most important is that the needs of the household are met.

> *Prayer:*
> *Lord, I pray for these marriages: may they always honor you. Get the glory out of their lives as they seek your face for answers during uncertain times. When they don't know what to do, help them regard the original marriage vows. I pray that another man will praise the way that they respect and cover one another (Proverbs 27:2). Let the stranger observe them and speak well of a union that is blessed by you. Thank you, Father that they are not self-absorbed by how many likes they get from Facebook, Instagram or Snapchat. May they carry Your presence and affect those who they encounter. And as they are influenced and inspired by other who held their mate in high regard, let it be spoken of them by others:* **"I don't know what it is, but they have something special from God."**

I Didn't Sign Up for This!

She never said it, but she entertained it a few hundred times. How long do you plan to be sick? I didn't sign up for this. How in the world did I end up with a disabled spouse? If a man doesn't work, he doesn't eat. ...And then, at the end of all her frustrations she said, "How long Lord"?

When you're dealing with a mate's illness that extends for a prolonged period of time, you have to show that you are committed to your spouse. You must be willing to adapt to the physical changes in their bodies; after all, you said, "in sickness and health". There's no time for you to jump out because your mate has cancer or some other terminal illness. Whether it be a physical disability or mental disability, or even when your mate is impotent and cannot perform sexual relations, remember, "in sickness and in health".

We learned a lot about ourselves during the days when COVID-19 burst on the scene. We heard and saw the disease spread. They reminded us daily of the loss of life that resulted from this disease. And when there was no known prescription, in the face of danger loved ones cared for one another. Many caretakers later found out that in taking care of others their own mental health had suffered greatly. I recommend that you assess what you are capable of. Know yourself and the ability that you have. You are capable of more than you know. Make sure that you are taking advantage of the moment to pull inventory on yourself, so that you can be a responsible husband or a responsible wife when the need arises.

You can't jump off the ship now!

- I mean, they didn't plan to get cancer.
- They didn't plan to have a terminal illness.
- Your husband didn't plan to be impotent.
- You didn't plan to have a female problem.
- You didn't plan to have any mental disabilities.
- You didn't plan for Alzheimer's or a stage of dementia.

Your mate didn't plan to be diagnosed with that! Neither did they envision nor sketch this out to trouble you, yet it has happened. As you have adjusted so well to other things, this also requires you to adjust. I empathize with all the imaginations that anyone would have to cast down during this time. Adjust your thinking so that the circumstance won't convince you that his sickness or hers are grounds for God to grant you a divorce. It is not.

It is a common, thing. (I Corinthians 10:13). People "do", have health challenges! And even though you are not the only one, the devil works overtime attacking your mind. If he could have his way, he would have you filled with self-pity. Your situation is not the only situation. You aren't the only one going through it. There are others having to endure the sickness of a mate, just as you are. I hear you saying, "man of God, health challenges are real". It's easier said then done, but you have to learn how to adapt. On those days when you are frustrated with the process, find someone you have watched care for their mate and allow them to pour into you. Receive from the grace and wisdom that they have walked in. You can do it with the right amount of love and patience. Frustration doesn't have to rule. You don't have to avoid coming home, staying out for extended hours just because you don't want to deal with it.

21

To Love and to Cherish

...Be Intentional

Love, protect and be careful to not put anyone before your mate. Your mate has to be more important than anyone else. Those whom you cherish and protect receive ultimate care from you.

So ought men to love their wives as their own body. He that loveth his wife loveth himself, for no man ever yet hated his own flesh, but nourished and cherisheth it, even as the Lord, the church

Ephesians 5:28-29

At the onset, during and throughout your mates' health challenge, be intentional. It is your duty. Paul gave reference in I Thessalonians 2:7, to the gentle nature of a nurse and how she cherisheth her children. He continued in vs 8, disclosing how affectionately desirous and willing he was to impart to the church. A husband's love towards his wife should be characterized by that same readiness to impart. His love towards his wife should be as gentle and affectionate. His desire should be to sow into his wife who he cherishes.

A nurse has a grace. A nurse comes to work every day. Their responsibilities include cleaning the patients. They may encounter cursing and spitting. Some are required to deal with blood. On any given day, they may be a assigned a patient who is prejudice. Nurses have a special grace indeed. Nurses are assigned patients from different religions. They have to be prepared for angry, disgruntled patients who refuse to get up and are not willing to go to rehab. Just as the nurse cherishes in adverse situations, so must husbands. To love and to cherish is to allow the all-sufficient grace to come upon you for your mate, even in adverse situations where you don't want to do it.

Lessons In Loving And Cherishing: What It Is Not!

Staying away from the home purposefully, too much, is not loving and cherishing. Spending time with single women or going on girls trips occasionally is alright. When you stay out too long, returning home just to get in the bed, that's not of God. Evidence that you need help is when you are avoiding the time factor. Cooking food for your mate and taking off, is not enough. It does not qualify as loving and cherishing.

Part of "Loving and Cherishing" is taking the time to still date the one you purposed to. Find an activity that both of you can engage in together. Things like walking and holding hands never grow old, said a wise brother. Be willing to give your spouse the undivided attention they need. Husbands, love her still. Cherish your wife as Christ loved the church, and as a nurse who works tirelessly dealing with the many adverse conditions in her patients. Neglecting to cherish (tend to, protect, hold in high esteem) can affect your mate in the areas of emotional and mental intimacy. How damaging is it for them to recognize that you don't care enough. They don't want to be passed off to a sister, a mother, nor your brother. The affection that they want from is you.

He that hath an ear, let him hear what the Spirit of the Lord is saying, "coming home late to avoid your mate, is not okay".

Cooking and cleaning and taking off for countless hours on Saturday is the kind of foolishness that needs to cease. It doesn't take that many hours to shop. The Holy Spirt knows what is hurting relationships and sheds light on things we can change to improve time spent in the company of your spouse.

Until Death, Do Us Part

Is adultery considered a death of the marriage? Yes, it is like a spiritual death.

When adultery takes place in a marriage, the marriage must be repaired. Take your pick. The relationship must be repaired. Trust must be restored. Even the individual who is affected by shame, embarrassment, and guilt will need healing. Counseling is not something that you can leisurely consider. You've got to receive counsel.

Proverbs 15:22 says, "Without counsel, purposes are disappointed, but in the multitude of counselors there is safety."

Adultery is a type of spiritual death to a marriage. The marriage relationship can't be properly repaired without the offending spouse experiencing remorse. Sex complicates your ability to think soberly when you are in the valley of decision. For some it is already hard enough to determine if they want to stay in the relationship or not. When a spouse has committed adultery, it's up to their husband or wife to decide whether to stay or leave. There are many motivations that influence what you choose to do.

Without remorse there is no indication of change. Without change, trust can't be repaired. David says, "I acknowledge my transgressions and my sinning is ever before thee," after committing adultery (Psalms 51:3). If that mate does not show any remorse, then his/her spouse has grounds for moving forward toward divorce.

Physical Death of a Spouse

When a person's spouse physically dies, he or she is at liberty to marry again.

The wife is bound by the law as long as her husband liveth; but if her husband be dead, she is at liberty to be married to whom she will: only in the Lord.

I Corinthians 7:39

Grounds for divorce is not an authorization for you to get married. I encourage you to seek the face of God how you are to proceed.

If An Unbelieving Spouse Depart

And the woman which hath an husband believeth not, and if he be pleased to dwell with her, let her not leave him. For the unbelieving husband is sanctified by the wife, and the unbelieving wife is sanctified by the husband: else were your children unclean; but now are they holy. But if the unbelieving depart, let him depart. A brother or a sister is not under bondage in such cases: but God hath called us to peace.

1 Corinthians 7:13-15

"If the unbelieving depart, let them depart for, you're not under bondage in such cases." If you're married to someone unsaved and they just want to leave you, that is a ground of divorce.

Abandonment

Abandonment occurs when your spouse moves out and you don't know where they are. You are uncertain about their whereabouts! You have no idea of where to locate them. If they are in town or moved to another state is unclear. Abandonment is grounds for divorce.

There are unbearable situations when a spouse should be cautioned about remaining in an unhealthy environment. One such situation is a spouse's addictions. The addiction can lead to both physical and mental abuse. In the case of an abusive wife or husband, the spouse should seek immediately help. Until special counseling is sought out and real change can be measured, separation would be the better route. Always consider in your decision making if the spouse wants to get help or not. Watch out for outside voices who intentionally desire to sow discord. Rather than making a rash decision or jumping out of the marriage at the first sign of trouble, seek God.

It is not in God's will for you to be continually oppressed and depressed for the rest of your life. God can heal and restore what both husband and wife are willing to reveal.

Imprisonment is another one of those delicate areas that demands that a spouse seek God, especially when the spouse has a lengthy prison sentence. Similar questions exist in this scenario also. Can this be worked out? If there is no repair or no remorse shown the spouse has no better route than to seek God as to how to procced.

Infidelity

Infidelity has many faces. It is not easy a for loyal spouse to continue once betrayal, unfaithfulness and breach of trust occur. The spouse committing the infidelity has committed a transgression. In deceit they have violated their mate's trust and caused them to be guarded and filled with skepticism. Don't have a leisurely attitude about counseling. It is a must.

Never make permanent decisions on temporary feelings. If the marriage can be helped, if the person desires counsel, then get some help. ...But if they don't show any remorse...

Remorse:

- *repentance, sorrow, deep regret, sadness) about something that was done.*

David's son Absalom, in his rebellion against David, never showed remorse. Even when he came around David and hugged David. If they were in the same city for two years, they never were around each other. Remorse ushers in change, a change that is not temperamental.

Thank you, for allowing me to minister to you as I must confess, God is not through with me yet. I listened to your responses, your acknowledgements, your comments even as the Holy Spirit dealt with some sensitive areas in my own life.

Some of you were stooped because of heaviness, while others said, "If only I'd had these teachings some time ago." Several of you mentioned sharing these teachings with those who are preparing to be married.

What you experience in marriage can be directly linked to teachings received under the tutelage of an anointed servant of God. I am experiencing a good marriage. This is due to years of teaching that my wife received while sitting under Pastor Brenda Timberlake and the late Bishop Mack Timberlake. When it was time for us to get married, the Holy Spirit had already prepared her. He that finds a wife, finds a good thing. These teachings are meant to enhance and add to what you already know. ...And yes, there are some things that you may have to unlearn that were bad and habit forming. May the Lord add to you more and more.

Father in Jesus' name Lord God, I thank you Father. Oh God, as you shared with me, Lord God, as I prepared these messages, that what you put in my spirit have been the prayers of some people for years, Lord God. I honor you for opening the doors and making the deposit in my spirit.

By your grace, You, oh God, have helped us unpack solutions to complex situations. You said, call upon Me, and I will answer you. You have answered us and shown us great and mighty things that we did not know. Father, I give you the glory for using me and for speaking those things to strengthen me as well. You chose to bless us, and I give you praise.

You said you will instruct us and teach struct us in the way that we should go. You promised to guide us with your eye (Psalm 32:8). Thank you for pouring out your wisdom. I declare over every marriage and all those desiring to be married that they will experience "next-level love", in Jesus' name, amen.

Loving Her as Christ Loved the Church

For the husband is the head of the wife even as Christ is the head of the church, and he is the savior of the body. Therefore, as the church is subject unto Christ, let the wives be to their own husbands in everything. Husbands love your wife, as Christ also loved the church and gave himself for it, that he might sanctify and cleanse it with the washing of water of the word, that he might present it to himself a glorious church, not having a spot or wrinkle, or any such thing; but that it should be holy and without blemish. So ought men to love their wives as their own bodies. He that loveth his wife, loveth himself. For no man ever yet hated his own flesh, but nourish, and cherish it, even as the Lord, the church. For we are members of the body of his flesh and of his bones. For this cause shall a man leave his father and mother and shall be joined to his wife. And they two shall be one flesh. This is a great mystery; but I am speaking concerning Christ and the church. Nevertheless let every one of you in particular so love his wife even as himself; and the wife see that she reverences her husband.

Ephesians 5:23 – 33

There's a Husband in Her House

If you don't know the meaning of a thing, there is potential for abuse or abnormal use! You cannot respond appropriately in a marriage relationship out of ignorance. For starters, a husband is a married man. A husband is a male spouse (significant other, better half, partner) to a wife. A husband is also a manager who stewards over a household. In relation to his wife, he is to cleave to her.

Cleaving speaks to the type of connection and attachment that is difficult when you have soul-ties with someone else. The man that you desire to marry and create a bond with, should not have to compete with your previous partners. It is almost impossible to connect with a potential husband when sexual soul-ties exist.

One of the common mistakes women make is believing that the soul-ties that existed in past relationships will dissipate once the vows are made at the altar. Husbands don't forget about the mother of their children, just as wives often carry the memory of their baby's father.

Overnight engagements are not advisable! It takes more than a mere two to three months of getting to know someone to jump into a lifelong commitment. There is no value in avoiding those personal questions regarding the relationship status of your mate's previous partner.

Trying to form a relationship on top of one that never ended or one that ended badly can prove disastrous. It is difficult to start something new when the person you are trying to connect with is pre-occupied with trying to get closure.

Is this a rebound relationship? Are there lingering emotional ties? Has there been recent physical contact that cause him or her to romanticize about the last time they were intimate? When was the last time?

His first response may be one of avoidance, making light of your question or shrugging his shoulders as if he can't remember. The timing might not be right to press the issue, but these are the sensitive questions that must be revisited. As much as you need to be truthful to him about the same, he needs to be truthful with you. Your intention is that his heart and yours will be truly prepared for one another.

The ideal engagement period is a time of commitment, making a mutual promise and yielding to the person you desire to be exclusive with. The preferred scenario is one where your fiancé is undivided in their affections toward you. Working through soul-ties emotionally and physically, is for the benefit of the relationship. The alternative would be you struggling with another woman in his system and he, competing with another man in yours.

The Man That God Makes

God makes a man who is responsible for his household. It is a God idea that he takes the leadership role in the house, which includes always honoring the significance that his helpmate brings to the family.

My prayer for men who never saw biblical manhood modeled is that you will allow God to show you how. Many households were governed by Big Ma or a strong dominant grandmother. Mamaw was usually the cook, the religious leader, and the disciplinarian in the house. She was the figure that held things together when her husband spent most of the day at work.

This God idea was seldom modeled, but it is nevertheless right. God made man to lead! He made man to take the leadership role and be faithful.

Whoso finds a wife finds a good thing and obtains favor from the Lord.

Proverbs 18:22

Even in a relationship, he wants God to be honored. He notices her after the time spent in prayer about a potential mate. He meets her and perceives her to be a blessing. He becomes aware of her nuances that make her who she is as they spend time together. He enjoys the way that they connect. They get along well. All his friends and family overhear him saying, "She's the one." The man has obtained favor from God. He recognizes that God has honored his heart's desire by sending him this beautiful addition and prepared him for it. He enjoys getting to know her until she manifests as his wife.

Give Me My Hadassah

Give me a woman like Hadassah, whose days of purification have been accomplished. That's the kind of woman that a godly man desires. A young lady who has gone through a process of removing or detaching from any contaminants. A woman who has had time to deal with her emotions, hurts, fear, who knows her value and worth. His delight is for a woman like Hadassah, who gave herself to seasons of myrrh and sweet odors. His appreciation is for the quality time she has spent being detoxed and being refreshed. Give me a Hadassah, a woman who spent quality time doing the work on herself (Esther 2:12).

Give Me Ruth

Give me Ruth, who was faithful in serving. The type of woman who is occupied and not idle. A man desires a woman like Ruth, who positioned herself, who's reputation proceeded him meeting her. Boaz spoke well of her, declaring that she was one who showed kindness. She was different in that she was known to not follow about young men, rich or poor. In the city, she was viewed as a virtuous woman. Give me my Ruth (Ruth 3:9-11)! A god-fearing man will always respond to the acts of kindness or a woman who presents herself in this way.

What Has He Ever Managed?

What does his track record look like? How does he react when unexpected things show up? The head of woman is man, but realistically, can he speak into her life? Every woman should want to know if a potential mate has the capacity to lead. She also needs to examine whether he has the type of character that enables her to submit to the role of wife and helpmate. Is he worth a second look? What does his track record look like? Did I ask that already?

Brothers, she really wants to know, and she doesn't want to second-guess herself. What have you ever been in charge of? These are just a few of her questions which she needs answered before she decides to connect. Her intention is to give her heart fully, to a man that has finished something. She needs to know that when things get intense or tough, he won't quit. Every sister and brother as well should have some degree of certainty before you begin to connect and give your heart fully.

Moreover it is required in stewards, that a man be found faithful.

I Corinthians 4:2

Husbands are required to be faithful to their wives. Faithfulness must be portrayed during the engagement period. It's important to be faithful to the agreements made between you and the person you are dating. There are important things to share, like are you dating exclusively?

Stewardship includes having the capacity to finish or complete what you started. Sister, you may be married to someone or at least know a brother who never finishes anything. They have a history of starts and stops! They excuse their way out finishing. They apologize for not having enough hours in the day. Somewhere along the way, he may have lost the enthusiasm and motivation that was there in the beginning. Zechariah 4:10, instructs us not despise the day of small beginnings… Completing what seemingly is a small thing is a victory.

Introspect, Reflecting, Taking a Closer Look

No one can take their life to the next level without taking responsibility for themselves. Every man needs to take inventory of himself as he begins to pursue a wife who God will charge to cover. This is equally important for women to take inventory of yourself before a young man pursues your hand in marriage.

But queen Vashti... Instead of looking inward to determine what motivated her response in refusing to come at the king's commandment by his chamberlains; therefore, was the king very wroth, and his anger burned in him. Her behavior towards her husband, the king, was strong enough to set a standard precedence in all the kingdom. The other women would view her stubborn, prideful, rebellious contempt and begin to act out in wrath towards their husbands as well.

Queen Vashti's behavior caused her to be forever banished from the presence of the king, and that the king should choose another queen worthier than she. Just as it was up to her to do the work, every woman must put in the time to deal with emotional triggers stemming from domestic abuse, daddy issues, rejection, or other issues. More often than not, the things women bury sabotage the success of the relationship.

Let the Words of My Mouth and the Meditation of My Heart

Ladies, you are connecting with a man, not a boy! If you can't control your tongue, you are not ready. There are things every man must put away if he desires to walk in the mantle of a husband. A woman must never speak to a man like she would speak to her son. If a woman has that kind of contempt for his behavior, she may need to rethink connecting.

The relationship demands changes in both the man and the woman. The moment inadequacies are detected the couple should adjust. In a healthy relationship, the couple that grows together will seasonally acknowledge levels of immaturity that will require some work.

When I was a child, I spake as a child, I understood as a child, I thought as a child: but when I became a man, I put away childish things.

I Corinthians 13:11

Men don't typically hold on to childish things. They go from puberty to a transitional adolescent stage where they not only change physically but develop cultural expressions and process things differently. It is during this period where most are willing to put away childish things.

Love Is Spelled "T-I-M-E"

As much as I want to take credit for that, it's something I learned from wife, who I affectionately refer to as "Grace Girl". **She is a manifestation of GRACE unto me.**

Time is fleeting. Except there be a divine intervention of God, it will never stand still. It is so precious that once it is gone, you cannot get it back. With time comes changes, some expected and some unexpected. We go from speaking one way to another. Our understanding changes as we become impacted by different influences. The way we process things begins to differ as our capacity to handle batches of new information. We grow in discernment and our awareness increases.

Our decisions are more deliberate than before. Men begin to think and understand in a way that causes them to consider how their words will land. Praise God for the man who is not haste with his words. He would never damage his woman. His words are responsible. He values his children and the high regard they have for what he says. Time matures all men who desire to be a better version of themselves.

"Lord help me to take heed to my ways."

Psalms 39:1

What an unusual request for David or any man to make. His desire was to monitor or set a watch over his tongue. He knew how important it was to be cautious with his words. He was willing to admit how frail he was. Because David understands the untimeliness of his own inconsistencies, he prostrates his heart before God.

Help me. Before I affect somebody negatively, help me. Help me to carry myself in such a way that my behavior will create an echo in the house. Let my wife and my children's interactions reflect what they see in me. This is the kind of manager I was referring to, one who sets the temperament in his house.

When your inability to process anger escalates, it usually results in "anger management issues." As steward of your house, anger becomes the echo in halls, bedrooms, and the family room. A husband who is short, abrupt, and rude in speech must deal with the consequences of the seeds he is sowing. That same anger shown unintentionally or not is now resonating through his wife who has been spiritually and emotionally affected.

The same is true when the husband models unforgiveness. Little does he know that the same resentment he is expressing will return to him once his wife is affected. As a manager, the husband's disposition creates reactions. He does not need to be born again to set the tone in the house. If the woman is born again, after provoking, fretting, fussing, constant belittling, she will retaliate.

There is a reason why I Peter 3:7, admonishes men to honor their wives. They are the weaker vessels. Husbands are to consider how delicate his wife is. He is to understand her to make necessary adjustments when handling or speaking with her. A husband's responsibility is to know how things emotionally impact his wife.

A man with a broken and contrite heart is willing to sacrifice. He willingly admits and turns from behaviors that negatively affect others. He is not perfect, but when something goes wrong, he acknowledges his role in the occurrence and repents. That's the man that leads his household. When they see him apologizing, the fruit or echo of his seed is a forgiving wife and forgiving children.

Ripples are created from the drop of one pebble. If a husband is a bad manager of finances, the ripples can be costly. If you create a pattern of bad financial decisions, those who you love will be affected. If you are frivolous with money, it can break your marriage. You are responsible for helping your children understand the value of a dollar. When you tithe, set up a saving account, sow seeds, establish an investment account, and operate from a budget, the echo will be less worry, less fear, and lying and holding back money. When a husband continues to make bad financial decisions the family's income is affected. If the couple initially decides on a joint account, the echo or result is oneness in their finances. "... Jesus declared, "For which of you intending to build a tower sitteth not down first and counteth the cost, whether he have sufficient to finish it?" (Luke 14:28).

While the earth remaineth, seedtime and harvest, and cold and heat, and summer and winter, and day and night shall not cease.

Genesis 8:22

- Seedtime represents a time of sowing, planting of the seed, tilling the ground.
- Harvest represents the crop or the gathering of it. It is the season of reaping.

The question is, when did you meet him? What season was he experiencing? Was he experiencing seedtime, or did you meet him in a season where he was harvesting what he had sown?

Does it seem like all hell is breaking loose? Are things happening that do not make any sense? You're struggling trying to figure out why carefully laid plans are failing flat. Both of you agreed on the job opening. Maybe you are trying to bid on a property or believing for financial increase to take a class next semester.

You called down favor and it seems like God is quiet. The message from church, entitled "Favor Ain't Fair" is not helping your situation. That's when you realize that you connected during a season of disfavor. Time would have revealed some important things about your husband, but you chose a short engagement.

Any number of issues could arise in your marriage because of the type of seed(s), he sowed during "seedtime". One example could be an unexpected illness due to a lack of regularly scheduled visits to a doctor. If your husband ignored those vendor invoices and did not reach out to settle delinquent accounts, it can affect the family's purchasing power. Another example can be mental health issues resulting from a whole slew of unresolved relationships including an absent father, an abusive mother, or an ex-lover who moved away with his child.

If your mate is experiencing a season of disfavor and suffering from commitment issues that go at least 10 years back, you may have difficulty bonding. There are drawbacks of connecting with a man during a season of disfavor. Overnight, microwave engagements and marriages do not stand a chance.

Even when the person is born-again, there is a season of beseeching God for mercy and grace to navigate that season when they are harvesting what they sowed.

"As Christ Loved" The Church
- Even as Christ loved
- Just as Christ loved
- The same as Christ loved
- A comparison for husbands to follow Christ
- Identical to how Christ loved
- Matching or measuring up to Christ's love
- In the same manner which Christ loved
- Characterized after the love that Christ displayed
- His relationship with the Church is to govern a husband's relationship with his wife.

There are going to be challenges in loving her as Christ loved the church. Confrontation, disagreement, and objections from within will try to give reasons why you should do otherwise. Husbands call into question the behavior of their wives saying, "But you don't know *my* wife." Drama will try and follow you without being invited. Despite that, men and women need to bring all past drama to an end.

Those lingering custody issues need to be resolved before you connect with a potential mate or even while you are married.

If you have a history of being provoked by your wife or the children's mother, I refer to you Jesus, the only one who ever did it right. Jesus will help you to be delivered from the things that are triggers when communicating with them, so that there won't be any disrespect. The Holy Spirit will give you words that protect your children's mother rather than harm her. Even when you are challenged, He will enable you to speak life.

Loving your wife even as Christ loves the church, includes bringing a closure to all financial challenges. Relationships that begin with a financial deficit must do the hard work of talking about money to avoid arguments. There is no comfort in living in a house where the foundation is built upon debt. Beloved, Jesus made references to a wise man which built his house upon the rock. When the rains descended and the floods came, and the winds blew, and beat upon that house; and it fell not: for it was founded upon a rock.

You can be anointed, operating in various gifts and still have a bunch of debt. That deficit is still something that you must contend with. This should be a priority in your relationship/marriage.

Christ loved the church. You loved Sally, Barb, and Louise. None of those ladies have ever given you as much trouble as the church has given Jesus. Not one of those ladies have had an agenda as different from the husband than the church and her agenda conflicting with Jesus.

What Do I Do with Old Things?

Old things they must be put behind you! The scripture declares, they shall come to the light. You must be intentional about putting behind things that have happened. The question is what does that process look like?

*For there is nothing covered, that shall not be
revealed, neither hid, that shall not be known.
Therefore whatsoever ye have spoken in
darkness shall be heard in the light; and that
which ye have spoken in the ear in closets shall
be proclaimed upon the housetops.*

Luke 12:2-3

Hebrews 4:13 says, that all things are naked before the
God, the eyes of God. Nothing is hidden from him.

There are things that need to be revealed about your past to
your spouse. There are things regarding your spouse's past that
need to be shared if connection is the goal. Depending on your
comfort level with that information, a background check may
be necessary. Remember, this is the person that you are
connecting with spiritually, emotionally, and physically. You
are taking the risk of connecting with them financially and may
consider having children with.

Do your diligence to find out things of importance before
the skeleton comes out of the closet. Do not shy away from
telling them that you need to know something concerning their
past. Let them know your uneasiness about what you might be
stepping into. Ask them about areas in their life that they still
need deliverance. Inquire about past partners to determine if
there is some sort of attachment remaining. Whatever advance
information you can obtain will help alleviate the pains of a
surprising divorce. Now is the time to get rid of your second
cell phone or your private cell phone line. Keeping secrets

from your wife is one of those "small foxes that eat at the root of the tree" (Song of Solomon 2:15-17).

Her Price

… Her price is far above rubies (Proverbs 31:10). Men are attracted to a virtuous woman. King Lemuel's mother told him what type of woman to look for. He was instructed to not look for a cheap and easy type of woman. Sister, you do not have to make yourself easy or cheap.

Sister, know your worth. Now is the time to begin to develop a Godly opinion of yourself. See yourself as value-added. You are a blessing. You are fearfully and wonderfully made. Divorce those negative words and mistreatments of the past. You do not have to be the pawn shop type girlfriend or the thrift store type girlfriend. You can choose to be the one on the showroom floor. Many sisters in the church have allowed the world to define "what a good man is, or what a good man looks like." As you begin to learn from the scripture what God requires of him, you can adjust the petition that you're requesting from God. As God begins to show you what is best for you, anything that comes your way that is not aligned with that will lose its ability to entice you.

You should have some idea of what you desire from the relationship. Before you connect you should know what type of lifestyle will make you comfortable. You want your mate to be responsible. Having a job is not a special quality. It is a given. Sister, you must be conscious of what is important to you in a relationship. Do you desire to connect emotionally? Are you interested in good conversation? If you know beforehand, you won't jump at the first suiter showing up demanding you to compromise.

There are levels of submission. Times of dating require both individuals to understand what level of submission will govern their relationship. This level of submission is often confused with the level of submission that's often expected during matrimony. Because the commitment level is different, requiring her to act or respond as one who is married is unrealistic.

Submitting to One Another

Biblical submission is not practiced in the households of many church goers. Etched in the minds of more than a few is the idea of being taken advantage of. If you did a survey, you would find married people who are one or two generations from parents who abused and took advantage of one another. What they experienced was one-sided submission.

Submission does not work automatically. Submission isn't spontaneous. It doesn't turn on right after you say, 'I DO." There's no better time for the process of submission to be implemented than at the point of engagement. And yes, it is a process, a series of steps that cannot be achieved all at once.

For the husband is the head of the wife, even as Christ is the head of the church; and he is the saviour of the body.

Ephesians 5:23

When we look at Ephesians 5:21, it all makes sense, "out of our reverence for Christ" we are to submit to one another. If only we could see and understand that this can only be done relationally (***depending on the level of the connection***). Because of our respect, regard, recognition, and regard for Christ we can function together "in relationship" without feeling enslaved. It is our gratitude to God that makes this painless.

Guide the House

---

*I will therefore that the younger women marry, bear children, **guide the house…***

I Timothy 5:14

Praise God for the obvious grace in the lives of women. It's easy submitting and respecting their abilities when you acknowledge their giftings. A helpmate is not relegated to just "certain areas", she is a high-functioning, "nobody-can-do-it-like-her" woman. Head of the household doesn't mean that you dominate over everything.

Wives are praiseworthy. God has blessed them with diligence, steadfastness, and determination. Wives are finishers. Wives follow through and are organized. They have capable hands that can be counted on. Husbands get tied up in unexpected projects, frustrated by something they did not get a chance to complete. Little did he know that his wife was proficient in getting it done, in less time.

Sir, it's going to work together for your good. When you submit to your wife, welcoming her know-how, the whole house benefits. Husbands can't be intimidated by the capacity their wives have to manage finances. She knows her way around a checkbook. She prioritizes household needs over wants when her husband may have a spending problem. Don't allow your household to be snared by debt. Receive the wisdom she operates in. Remember, two is better than one.

Guide (attend to be responsible for, give advice, supervise) the house. Going to the grocery store can be a different experience when a wife goes. My wife can go to the grocery store with $200.00 and get the same amount of grocery that I spent $300.00 for when I went. Rather than just putting stuff in the baskets, as managers they are thinking about tomorrow, next week, and next year. Wives know how get to it done. They don't go to the grocery store hungry but carries a list of household needs and coupons. You haven't had time, but she's been watching the price of certain items and knows the best time and the right quantity to buy.

Capacity to Love

Some have made the decision to marry an unbeliever. Their spouse is unsaved. He doesn't have the capacity to love you as Christ loved the church. He can love you and you can have a good marriage. Without the Spirit of Christ in him though, he doesn't have the ability to give you unconditional agape love. For a husband to love like Christ, he must have a born-again experience with Christ first.

Capacity to Love II

Unequally yoked can include connecting with someone who may be in a different season than you. Their spiritual level may be undeveloped. Give them time to become God conscience. Give them space to develop a prayer life. The sacrifice is an extended engagement. While God is working in his life, the same God is preparing you to live peaceably with him without frustration or regret. Sow an additional year and watch God season your speech with grace and with salt that you will know how to answer him.

Capacity to Love III

For to be carnally minded is death but to be spiritually minded is life and peace, because the carnal mind is enmity against God. It is not subject to the law of God. Neither indeed can be.

Romans 8:6-7

Is it possible to be anointed in gifting and yet immature in character? Ask the sister who sat across the table from a gift that she admired, but a man who lacked character. Ask the brother who was enamored with the "prophetess" who proved to be immature in the area of the soul, undeveloped in the intellect and was subject to poor decision making. You can be gifted and still need deliverance from past pains.

With our spirit man, we fellowship with God. With our spirit we have a sense of what is right or wrong. Through the soul (mind, will, emotions) we communicate with those around us. When you are connecting with carnal or undeveloped spiritual believers, there are going to be challenges. Prepare yourself for times of frustration. Things won't happen in them soon enough. As much as you want to see them filled with the Holy Ghost and speak in tongues, impatience with show up. You may want them to attend church more frequently. You may desire for them to see the significance of bringing their tithe into the storehouse, to no avail.

May the Clock Be Rewound

If they're not developed in Christian character, it's best to turn the clock back! Rewind the situation. You are attempting to connect to someone who is struggling similar to how you struggled when you were a babe in Christ.

Brothers, you aren't bound to the blueprint drawn up by your older brothers, or uncles who did it wrong. You deserve something better. Don't settle for a shot-gun wedding. Just because things were modeled before you there is no obligation on your part to repeat. I love my father and my grandfather. They're no longer here, but I saw some things modeled wrong. You must accept when they are wrong.

Remember ye not the former things, neither consider the things of old. Behold, I will do a new thing: now it shall spring forth; shall ye not know it? I will even make a way in the wilderness, and rivers in the desert.

Isaiah 43:18-19

Father,

Do something different in me. Break the chains.
Remove any loyalties with the patterns modeled
before us. Lord, heal our memory. I pray that we
won't consider the patterns. We are open for a new
thing. Let it spring forth now. Show those who are
having wilderness experiences, rivers in the desert.

In Jesus' name, Amen.

It's renovation time! The prophet is giving notice to that which needs to be torn up, ripped out and thrown away. Renovate means to restore. If the way your father treated your mother didn't work, what makes you think that the results will be any different in your household with your wife? Allow God to design your marriage. Let him create a checklist for you, including His original plans for marriage.

It is time for some upgrades. This is a season for old things to go from one state to a better state. Repairs, changes, and upgrades are on the way. God says, "trust me to help you make the adjustments and the improvements in your life.

That he might sanctify and cleanse it with the
washing of water by the word.

Ephesian 5:26

50

Husbands are required of God to sanctify or set his wife apart by the washing of the water of the word. There is nothing faulty about God's plan (blueprint). It is important who you connect with. Only a man of God, one that is saved or born again can do that successfully, minister next level love.

My wife corrected me about a year and a half ago, saying, "Why don't we have family devotion including the kids?" Thank God for her sensitivity. The Holy Spirit used her to nudge me and now we break spiritual bread together. The washing of water by the word is sanctifying my household. Just as Jesus trained the disciples, I am following suit by using the word which edifies, washes, and sets her apart.

that he might present it unto himself a glorious church, not having spot or wrinkle or any such thing; that it should be holy and without blemish.

Ephesians 5:27

It is important that all wives understand that she should be holy and without blemish. Husbands need to understand their wives more than anyone. Your knowledge of your wife should exceed what her family knows. She may have girlfriends that have grown up with her. They may know her entire life. They may have an advantage over you because of more information. They know about her hurts, her pains, her fear and concerns. Your work is cut out for you. You are charged, to "present her back to you" a glorious wife, a holy woman of God, not having spot wrinkle or blemish.

If we don't understand our wives, we won't be able to detect the meaning of that recent emotional outburst, for example. Our request should be that God would make us better listeners to her. James admonishes us to be swift to hear, and slow to speak. It doesn't help matters when you get angry when you don't understand your wife's point of view. Most men have had a time or two when their lack of concern caused them to ignore or tune out their wives. Interrupting them mid-stream only confirmed your impatience in an area that you perceived to be a short-coming.

Peter matured. His season of cutting off ears ceased. There were undeveloped areas in Peter's life, but he did not stop developing in character. Christ intervened on Peter's behalf. You too can intervene on behalf of your wife. Some things are seasonal. Believe God that she like Peter will transition out of some behaviors with prayer and a godly response from you.

Your Ear or Theirs

Wives need their husbands to listen. If you don't listen, by default they will turn back to their family members, and their girlfriends. Maybe they will offer her some advice. Because she could not turn to you for relief, she will seek out the counsel of an available listening ear.

When you could have listened, you didn't. Husbands feel indifferent when their wives are disclosing matters (personal) to outsiders. In this instance the husband chose not to hear. A pattern of this behavior evolves in counseling sessions where a mediator is necessary.

*So ought men to love their wives as their own
bodies. He that loveth his wife loveth himself.
For no man ever yet hated his own flesh, but
NOURISHETH and **CHERISHETH** it, even
as the Lord the church.*

Ephesians 5:28-29

*Nor of men sought we glory, neither of you, nor
yet of others, when we might have been
burdensome, as the apostles of Christ. But we
were gentle among you, even as a nurse
CHERISHETH her children: So, being
affectionately desirous of you, we were willing
to have imparted unto you, not the gospel of
God only, but also our own souls, because ye
were dear unto us. For ye remember, brethren,
our labour and travail: for labouring night and
day, because we would not be chargeable unto
any of you, we preached unto you the gospel of
God. Ye are witnesses, and God also, how holily
and justly, and unblameably we behaved
ourselves among you that believe.*

I Thessalonians 2:6-10

Jesus used a reference through the Apostle Paul to talk
about nourishing and cherishing your wife as Christ nourished
and cherished the church. A husband nourishes his wife by
providing her with the substances that are necessary for her

growth, mental, physical, and emotional health, and good condition. In nourishing his wife, he does as much as possible to provide her with a balanced state of mind.

Nourish her. She needs the provision that God has put in you to provide for her even if she is battling depression. This depression may have laid dormant in her soul before you came along. You might be partially responsible for her feeling this way. We acknowledge that you are not a medical doctor, but she is YOUR wife. Do your best to provide for your own (I Timothy 5). Provide the substance for her. Talk to your wife. Find out what she is dealing with. Listen to her and the Holy Spirt to diagnose the situation. Do not allow a hospital attendant from the operating room to be more longsuffering than you are to your own wife. Be patient and brace yourself for whatever she communicates. This might be emotional, mental, physical, or psychological.

These nurses are solution oriented. They go beyond the simple act of solving the problem. They are good listeners who are committed and disciplined.

1. What happened to you?
2. What's going on with you?
3. What have you been through?
4. Let's, let's get you healed.

That's what Christ did for the church. That's exactly what we are admonished to do. Love them as our body. You would not slap yourself. You wouldn't knock yourself upside the head. You would not cuss and use abusive words on yourself. You wouldn't physically, emotionally, nor mentally beat your wife down.

Rather than walking out of the house toward your mama's house, after acting like a fool, you would stay home. You would desire your wife to stay with you and understand you. These same seeds should be shown toward your wife. You must love her as your own body.

Choose not to be selfish financially. Why would you walk around with expensive shoes when your wife doesn't have any clothes? Every husband should be considerate of the personal undergarments that his wife needs. Don't purchase the high price, name brand tennis shoes when there are other needs.

Men, you cannot love your wife as Christ loved the church without the Spirit of God. Jesus told Nicodemus, "...you must be born again." Men, to reach the fullness of the capacity of next level love or the type of agape love that God has ordained for marriages to walk into, you can't do it outside of a relationship with Jesus Christ. You cannot sanctify your wife with the washing of the water of the word without being born again.

We extend an invitation to you, those who have not been born again. Those of you who need to surrender your heart to Jesus know who you are. There are some even who need to rededicate your life to Christ today. I'm going to pray a prayer of repentance and you're going to repeat after me if you desire to give your life to Christ. This is your moment of visitation. You that want the fullness of what God has poured out, just lift your hands right now. Brothers and sisters, repeat after me:

Jesus,

I acknowledge that I am a sinner in your sight. I repent of my sins. I ask you to forgive me. I don't have the ability to do what the prophet has said. I need your Spirit to help me to better my household. Jesus, come into my heart, as my Lord and Savior, I confess with my mouth and believe in my heart that God has raised Jesus from the dead. I confess I am saved.

Men or women, if you prayed that prayer, welcome to the family of God! Get into a Bible-based Christian church and allow yourself to grow in Christ. Get a plan for your family and let God show you how to be a better husband or a better wife. Let God show you how to take each other to next level love.

God bless you.

Respect Must be Shown and Earned

"Respect must be shown and earned" was accompanied by a puzzled look. "Lord that's like a contradiction", I said. Your Word says, "wives, submit or respect your husband." And even though I wasn't convinced, God didn't change the title of this chapter.

With little hesitation, I proceeded to ask, "Lord, why did you give me that title?"

As I reasoned, the Lord began to break down some things to me. He emphasized that both men and women have been damaged in previous relationships and previous marriages. He highlighted the many men and countless women who were brought up in households where there was no male authority. These households were managed by mothers, grandmothers, or an aunt, who could have been damaged.

When a woman enters a marriage, damaged, she doesn't have the capacity to honor her vows. She enters a relationship, exhausted and triggered by past experiences. In her attempts to move forward she finds herself depleted of the ability to submit to her husband. Even her good intentions and her efforts fall short. Because her heart is so guarded, she can't respect her husband. Part of her internal dialogue (non-verbal communication) includes, "I'm not going to allow anyone else to hurt me." Until women allow themselves to get healed of previous pains and previous hurt, they're not going to be able to do what the scripture says.

So many have skimmed over Ephesians 5:21 and come up with an idea that is not correct.

It says, "Submitting yourselves one to another in the fear of God." Verse 22 says, "Wives, submit yourself to your own husbands as unto the Lord."

Paul's ministry to the church of Ephesus in chapter 5 began like this: "Be ye therefore followers of God as dear children."

Those two verses are making a shift. What I mean by that is when Paul wrote to the Church of Ephesus, when he began to start chapter 5, he said, "Be ye therefore followers of God as dear children." He shifts and conveys a message to husband and wives in vs 21 and 22. There is a submission to "one another" to serve one another out of respect for Christ. The apostle then addressed what submission looks like in a household.

The husband's submission and respect to his wife does not validate "two heads of a household nor two heads of a ministry. While the man and the woman can both operate the pastor office, there exist only one head.

Even though a ministry gift can be in a body with the woman being the pastor or the man being the pastor, they're not two heads. There will always be one head, even though both have ministry gifts.

Take a look at vs. 23-25. "For the husband is the head of the wife, even as Christ is the head of the church, and the savior of the body." Therefore, as the church is subject unto Christ so let the wives be to their own husbands in everything.

Husbands, love your wife even as Christ also loved the church and gave Himself for it."

Lord, Help a Brother Out!

God calls a husband to submit to loving his wife as Christ loved the church. This commandment has proven to be hard to follow.

If a brother is not submitted to Christ, he cannot! If the brother is not submitted to the word of God, (ideas, beliefs, and ways of behaving), he cannot! If a woman marries a man, who isn't saved or who recently gave his life to Christ, he cannot! After being saved for 30 years, she cannot expect that young convert to be ready. Even though he is in Christ, he hasn't so soon adjusted to the requirements of this new life. To follow the pattern, set by Christ, he needs time for God to work on his character. His mindset, his skill set, and his ability to treat you like Christ loved the church isn't possible, yet. You either chose him or allowed yourself to be chosen. You placed yourself in a position of submission and respect, based upon the choice you made.

Why Are You Mad?

She seems upset! She knows that according to the scripture, the husband is the head of the wife, even as Christ is the head of the Church. She appears to be unsettled and frustrated with whether her husband can actually lead her. Her attempts to trust and be subject to him hadn't worked. ...And to make matters worse, she's wrestling with respecting the husband that she said yes to.

> *That he might present, sanctify and cleanse it*
> *with the washing of water by the word. That he*
> *might present it to himself a glorious church,*
> *not having spot, or wrinkle, or any such thing;*
> *but that it should be holy and without blemish.*
>
> *Ephesians 5:26-27*

What is it that you desire in a relationship? There are some things that you must be willing to forgo, or opt out of. Matrimony becomes a lifelong commitment when you allow God to prepare you for it! Are you willing to wait on a man of God who knows God and His word? Are you willing to wait until God reveals to you a bride, who's inward beauty exceed her outward adornments? There are some things that are worth waiting on.

God will work! Sisters, allow God to do a work in your future husbands. Allow God to mature him, and give him the capacity to cleanse and wash his family during family devotions and fellowship. Give God a moment to develop him so that he can recognize any blemish and be a good steward over his family. Brothers, allow your future bride to become more God conscience. A wife that knows God, knows how to honor her husband and respond to his needs. I pray that those who haven't married yet allow God to "have at your mate."

Lord, Help a Brother Out! II

Christ was the example. "There was no guile in Him". Pilate said, "I find no fault in this, man (John 19:4). A husband should strive to be an example of Christ. He should strive (make great effort) to be the exact, the brightness of his glory, bless his name, the express image of his person before his wife and before his children (Hebrews 1:3). Sisters, you have need of patience! His capacity for being this example in various areas of his life is not there yet. Don't get upset with your spouse. Trust God's process. Don't allow your feelings to challenge or suspend what God can do over time.

Colossians 3:18 says, "Wives, submit yourselves unto your own husband as it is fit in the Lord."

"As it is fit in the Lord" is not an option. There is no acceptable alternative. God does not acknowledge your partial obedience. Submission is the right thing to do.

God has designs on how your household is to be. God has dibs on how your relationship is to govern. He claims the right to choose what is right for His children, over others who don't know now what is best.

The word submit is considered a cuss word in the church. How the church can categorize the word submit with bad language or profanity is beyond me. Most would rather use the word cuss rather than curse. These words are used interchangeably. Both are used for wishing misfortune or relaying ill feelings on another. Some women consider submission a cussing word. It is associated with a bad or evil word because it requires you to do something sometimes that you don't want to do, or something that you never saw modeled.

I Delivered Them Unto You

> *Be ye followers of me, even as I also am of Christ. Now I praise you, brethren, that ye remember me in all things, and keep the ordinances, as I delivered them to you. But I would have you to know, that the head of every man is Christ; and the head of the woman is the man; and the head of Christ is God.*
>
> *I Corinthians 11:1-3*

The advantage is ours. He delivered it to us. He knew that there was no way we could operate out of ignorance. He purposefully said, "But I would like you to know that the head of every man is Christ, and the head of the woman is the man, and the head of Christ is God."

> *Every man praying or prophesying, having his head covered, dishonoreth his head. But every woman that prayeth or prophesieth with her head uncovered, dishonoreth her head: for that is even all as she has been shaven. She is to be covered. The woman needs a man to cover her.*
>
> *I Corinthians 11:4-5*

Verse 8 says, "For the man is not of the woman, but the woman for the man."

The value of these scriptures emphasizes the importance of making sure that before yielding your "yes" to a brother, you are assured that he is a follower of Christ and hears from God. My pastor, is often heard quoting the words of Bishop Otis Locket, "If you want your wife to follow your leadership or your wife to submit or to respect you, make sure she knows that you can hear from God and get the answers needed for the family.

Sister don't be shy about yielding to trustworthy authority before getting engaged to a man. Bring him before them. They may be able to help or offer counsel when you have missed something. Prayerfully there is someone in your circle who is wise enough to discern if you should proceed or to tell you, {"Wait,"} or to tell you, "I got a witness with him."

If your parents are not trustworthy authority, and are not sober enough to make a spiritual judgment or decision, you should not bring before them the man pursuing your hand in marriage. Brothers, look before you leap. Make sure you usher her before trustworthy authority. A little caution is better than a lifetime of regret.

Your pastor or a maybe a woman of God who has served as a mother figure may be able to see what you can't. Allow your potential mate to dialogue, spend some sessions in the company of sharing his or her intentions. The nature, the values, the motives, the way a person thinks, decides and forbears can be revealed during time(s) of prayer or over lunch with your pastor or mother figure. There are things that God will reveal that are not obvious to anyone else. Don't allow your emotions to win out. It was Dr. Myles Munroe, who said, "One of the greatest hindrances to spiritual discernment is our emotions."

Young girls are conditioned from a very young age to except the narrative of growing up, marrying a prince, and living in a beautiful mansion. Today women, young and old, are in love with the idea of being married, way before a man shows up. They have already imagined their honeymoon. They have already picked out their wedding dress. Some have been asked repeatedly about setting a date. Without shame, people bring them names of possible suitors, telephone numbers and email addresses that serve to work up their emotions.

If you place yourself in a position of being in love with the idea of being married, it's easier for you to ignore the red flags (reservations) of a man that does not follow Christ. You ignored the warning signs and allowed yourself to believe that he was saved, even with the absence of spiritual fruit in his life.

When a man's heart is set on having you, he can appear to be religious. He pretends by acting to be spiritual. He claims to be spirit-filled long enough to entice you in a moment of weakness. Women use the same deceptive tools to woo a man to bed. Wanting to have intercourse is not reason enough to connect with a person. Countless women ended up in bad relationships because they had sexual relations before allowing the men to come before trustworthy authority to check his spirit.

One of the Greeks definitions of the word 'submission' is "hupotassō". It means to be under someone else's authority. The Latin word for 'respect' is respectus, which means to look. The prefix, [re] can means to do something again. A person does not submit to another mistakenly. When a person looks to you and respect you, it's on purpose. For a wife to walk in submission, it is not without effort. She understands relationally how God has set man and honors his significant role in her life. Remember I Corinthians 11:3 – The head of man is Christ, and the head of the woman is man...

Sisters, you should not respect (regard, honor, give recognition) to a man who does not add value to you. If a man cannot add value to you, it will be challenging to respect him. It seems like in this day and time, men must earn respect. This is the attitude of a sea of women.

Likewise, ye wives be in subjection to your own husbands; that, if any obey not the word, they also without the word be won by the conversation of the wives. While they behold your chaste conversation coupled with fears. Whose adorning let it not be that outward adorning of plaiting of the hair, and of wearing of gold, or of putting on apparel, but let it be the hidden man of the heart, in that which is not corruptible, even the ornament of a meek and quiet spirit, which is in the sight of God is a great price.

I Peter 3:1-4

Take a Look in the Mirror

The mirror is a looking glass. It does not create the image but is a reflector of what's before it. Some women would argue against it, but the qualities, personality traits, and characteristics listed in I Peter 3:1-4 are missing in their lives.

This is not an attack on women although some would beg to differ.

A wife must, in position to her husband, have a meek and quiet spirit. These Christ-like strengths are rare because of the verbal damage, the physical damage, the sexual damage and the damage that resulted from seeing her mother and/or grandmother damaged. If you are damaged in certain areas, your vocal response of anger and defense is the result.

You're always going to feel like you must challenge authority if the authority you submitted to before, damaged you. The alternative is allowing God to heal you! Psalms 147:3 says, "He healed the broken in hearted, and he bindeth up their wounds." If you don't get healed from the previous relationship, you will punish, vent, or take it out on this new innocent person, who could be the right person.

Paul prayed to God that your whole spirit, soul, and body be preserved blameless (I Thessalonians 5:23).

With your spirit you connect, do ministry, and have continual rapport with God. To exist in a marriage, your soul (mind, will, intellect) and all your mental capacities must be engaged. This is about relationship! It only works when you communicate with your mate. If there is pre-existing damage in areas of your life before you met him or her, you're going to enter a marriage depleted of the ability to give of yourself. You won't be able to emotionally connect. It's worth getting the healing you need now! ...Otherwise, you could literally, run the right person away. Don't make what could be a blessing a curse by rehashing and regurgitating what was done in the previous relationship.

Acting Out of Character

An evangelist who I respected went off. People began to judge her for acting out of character. I had no issues with the teaching I heard ministered from time to time. Instead of going along or siding with what others were thinking, I decided to seek God for myself. The Lord said she was damaged. The evangelist later revealed how she was damaged in previous relationships with men and with women as well. She was doing great spiritually with God and flowing in the gifts. It wasn't until someone got close to the area that she was damaged in that triggered her.

Indeed, her behavior was out of character, but it did not disqualify her from being a woman of God. Like others, however, there were areas of her life that were suppressed, and healing was needed.

What's Up with All the Disrespect?

Why do wives disrespect their husbands? Why do wives disobey the command given from the word of God to **RESPECT** their husbands? What cause wives to reason and struggle with doing relationship the way that God said it? Among those reasons is the influence of disgruntled woman who are publicized on reality tv. shows. These programs are filling women with all kinds of crazy thoughts. These women think that they can take over households and talk to a man in a degrading way. As a woman of God, you have to be responsible for what goes in your ear and eye gates. You should never talk to a man in a way that reduces him like he's your son. This is one of the biggest mistakes that is made by so many women.

He is not your son, and you are not his momma! Brothers have literally put themselves in a position of sonship by addressing his wife as mama. In days when men did not talk much, they would respond to a question or a decision with "whatever mama says." That's not what the Bible says. When mama began to talk, dad or grandpa just said, "Uh-huh. Uh-huh." He placed himself in a position of sonship, and that's what we saw. That's why a lot of men don't know how to be a leader nor operate in authority over the household. It is because they never saw it modeled before them.

Another reason for the lack of respect for husbands is wives don't find him to be dependable. If she cannot depend on him to be there for her, physically and emotionally, she will begin to literally go to someone else. Wives desire to express themselves and be vulnerable toward their husband without judgment. She wants her husband to listen to her and be sensitive to her needs. A wife wants to know that her husband is reliable and trustworthy for her.

Among the things that husbands can do if they desire a wife to be submissive is build a track record. This is true, especially if a woman has been damaged in a previous relationship. Once the husband develops a track record, that would facilitate the process of her healing. While she should have come into the relationship whole and healed, many women do not. Brothers don't rush what you are not ready for. Now that you are married and want to continue, you must be willing to put in some work. To her, it's what he does, not what he says. Her defenses may be up until she sees a difference between her husband and the guy(s) that hurt in the past. Her breakthrough often is predicated on her husband's initiative to be a provider, a protector, and someone who can naturally and spiritually nourish her.

Some women do not respect the healing process. They convince themselves that they could move on to a new relationship without taking care of their own mental health. It's no wonder she responds like she does when she sees the same characteristics in her husband as those she saw in the abuser. She made certain vows like "never again will I subject myself to that". It's no wonder that she comes out like a wildcat swinging. Every time the wrong buttons are pushed husbands will see a familiar emotional response of a woman in pain.

A woman loves a confident man! When a woman doesn't believe that you're confident in what you do and how you lead her, she begins to lose respect. When husbands are not confident, many women "take the lead". As crazy as this sounds, before the ship sinks, somebody needs to step up to the plate.

Don't Jump Ship

Lord, help us so that we will value the position that you have put us in. He us to see it more than just a role, a function, or something we do just to pass time. Lord, help us to commit ourselves as men even during times of difficulty.

In viewing the movie, The Titanic, I was blessed by the captain. He did not jump off the ship. Instead, he went down with the ship. He did not leave his post. As the captain stood in harm's way, so should husbands stand in the gap and be there through thick and thin. One thing my wife says to me that women find confident men sexy. They find it assuring when a man is confident, when a man has the moto, "I got you."

A woman respects a man who is a man of humility. She respects a man humble enough to know his limits and his abilities. She has great respect for the man who knows when he needs help and is open for correction. When her husband acknowledges in a situation, the God given insight that his wife has, he is esteemed in her eyes.

Wives are in some areas sharper than their husbands. They can be smarter and can have a capacity level for things that cannot be matched by their husbands. A husband can recognize his wife's strength and benefit from all that she adds to him, being that they are on the same team.

Likened to the CEO of a company benefiting from the chief financial officer, the secretary, the parliamentarian or the treasurer. Consider the association of a president with the joint chief of staff. Because they are on the same team, the president greatly benefits from the firsthand knowledge that the joint chief of staff can offer due to his or her military expertise.

Wives never want to be perceived as a liability but as an asset. She is not interested in being "STRONG-ER". A God-fearing woman will never fall into error by competing and comparing herself to her husband. The scripture says it is unwise.

Family traditions (beliefs, customs, expressions, attitudes, and ways of thinking) have robbed women of their desire to submit to their husbands. These traditions are the norm in their family. It's what everyone knows, has seen and what has been accepted. Mark 7:6-9, emphasizes the strength of "holding the traditions of men" and how they make the word of God of none affect.

As a little girl, if you were raised around a domineering mother or a domineering grandmother, their expressions, and ways of handling and mishandling situations can be a significant resistance to submitting to men or husbands. It's up close and personal. You see women usurping their authority all the time. The reality shows are a contributor. Some of these women come up in an environment where they were raised around a passive father or a passive man that allowed a woman to dominate him. Such was the case with Jezebel and King Ahab. Jezebel entered matrimony damaged emotionally. She did not have the ability, nor desired the ability to submit to Ahab. Jezebel was damaged. Her previous experience played out in the new relationship.

Dominant Women in Christian Settings

Big Momma, Memaw, Nana, are names we affectionately refer to grandma. She wasn't exempt from trouble but she never game up. She was "a good Christian", but was domineering nevertheless. And because grandma modeled, mothers adapted. This narrative is so common, though it may not be your story. Big Ma's around the world were central in the family. She was a key figure that held the family together. It was her strength and no nonsense that kept things in order.

If a woman has been damaged in a previous or present marriage, her ability to trust and capacity to trust are amongst those things that must be restored. If he cheated, the foundation of trust must be built all over again. When you break trust, especially in the case of adultery, you have already broken the covenant. That trust level must be repaired. No one knows what he is capable of like you. No one knows what he has done before and that's why trusting him is such a challenge for you.

Marrying a man with whom you are unequally yoked will present challenges. II Corinthians 6:7-14, warns us. "Don't be unequally yoked together with unbelievers. "For what fellowship hath righteousness with unrighteousness?" What communion has dark with light? What concord hath he that believeth with an infidel?"

So, Paul gives you a warning! You're not going to be able to fully submit to somebody that you can't communicate with. Submission is painful when the man you marry is not submitted to the word of God. When a man who is spiritually immature marries a woman who is a little more seasoned, challenges can occur due the different levels of spiritual understanding.

Romans 8:6-8, says, "The carnal mind is not subject to the law of God." "Neither indeed can be." When a man is very young, in the Lord, he has a carnal mind in a lot of areas. He couldn't possibly be submitted to the word of God. ...And while you are fully submitted and willing to do everything that God tells you, remember, it was you who decided to marry him. Remember your decision when the consequences come. These are the consequences that you have created!

Father, In Jesus' name, I thank you for your wisdom. I thank you for giving me the knowledge to give your people. I pray that their eyes of understanding have been enlightened. Bring your word back to remembrance. As you have ushered them into change, use them to share this word with others. Thank You for providing advanced information for decision making in the futures.

Posturing Yourself with the Spirit of Ruth

Ruth has what you have. She has times and she has seasons. Her story begins one way and ends in another. Ruth will tell you: things don't always stay the same. Today turns into tomorrow, and yesterday becomes ashes. You may identify with her in one season, and you may not identify with her in another. Ruth's seasons had purpose, despite her feelings and reactions toward some of the events that happened. Similarly, some seasons we come up against or encounter something unexpectedly that makes no sense to our natural mind. So, we ask ourselves: "What do we do when it just doesn't make sense?"

What She Wasn't Doing Was Putting On Airs

And Boaz answered and said unto her, It hath fully been shown me all that you have done unto thy mother-in-law since the death of thine husband: and how thou hast left thy father and thy mother and the land of thy nativity, and art coming to a people which thou knewest not heretofore. The Lord recompense thy work, and a full reward be given thee of the Lord God of Israel, under whose wings thou art come to trust.

Ruth 2:11-12

Who can find a virtuous woman? For her price is far above rubies.

The heart of her husband doth safely trust in her, so that she shall have no need of spoil.

She will do him good and not evil all the days of her life.

Proverbs 31:10-12

Proverbs 31:1 says, "The Words of king Lemuel, the prophecy that his mother taught him." Many women conferences have had Proverbs 31 as its theme. Women around the world have jumped and shorted, worship and cried after being ministered to from this chapter. It's almost as if God put the scripture in the Bible, just for them. It is no strange thing that most women in the church have taken ownership over it. What surprised me was this letter to King Lemuel, was from a prophecy that his mother chose to teach him.

This letter was designed to teach men!!! I won't say that women stole this chapter. I will say, that women borrowed it and put it among their stuff. This entire chapter is about a man's mother schooling (educating, instructing) him: **"WHAT TYPE OF WOMAN DO I LOOK FOR?"**
It's our turn! What women took from men has been restored to us to use it.

Naomi is a stoic figure in the life of Ruth. She represents a person who can endure hardness without disclosing her pain to everyone. Her real-life experiences and her reactions to them enabled her to school Ruth. Ruth observed Naomi and the particular way she navigated inconveniences that caught her by surprise.

Posturing is an attitude. Too many difficult days in a row can break you. Those that don't succumb have a different outlook on the other side of the test. They are changed forever because they didn't break.

Posturing has to do with the positioning of something. The posturing of the body is obvious, whether one is sitting or standing. The way you posture yourself is a way that you can mislead a person or a way that you can impress a person.

Naomi was not putting on airs! Ruth had learned from the best. The fruit never falls too far from the tree. Now Ruth is walking about with a unique posture. She has the attitude and that extra something that gets the attention of others. It was all in her approach. It was all in her positioning toward Boaz that got his attention.

You Don't Look Like What You've Been Through

You don't have to wear your grief on your sleeve. Before Ruth encountered or met Boaz, she suffered the death of her husband, Mahlon. This was reason enough to grieve. In addition, there was family hardship. Ruth's sister-in-law, Orpah, lost her husband Chilion. Her mother-in-law was also widowed due to the passing of her husband, Elimelech (Ruth 1:1-5).

She saw three deaths: two sons and their father. Ruth was well acquainted with grief. She had experienced bad days in her life. She had to push through the imaginations that accompanied the famine in that area. And after all this, she believes to see a better day. If anybody can turn this "thing" around, the God that Naomi introduced me to can. Ruth was determined to step into a new season.

Some of you can relate to losing a spouse to death. Others may have gone through a divorce or a painful breakup with a boyfriend. Time and chance happen to us all. Your girlfriend, or a wife could have passed. The "dis-ease" of losing someone who has sown so much in your life can be unbearable. Your heart, your body, soul, and spirit don't know how to react to this loss. Because it's a loss, an individual may have to go through a transitional period where he or she needs God's grace and strength. May the words of Joel 2:25-26 resonate in your ears: God can restore the years that the cankerworm, the locust, and the palmy worm have eaten. You can believe God in the new season to restore some things that you lost. You cannot lose hope in trusting God. I know firsthand of the grace that's needed after suffering emotional, psychological, mental, and spiritual trauma.

A Decree Born Out of Pain

Pain provokes. I was stirred as I sat with the thing that came to afflict me. I sat with it long enough that I began to give occasion to the wrong thoughts that turned into words. I was done. I declared over my life that I was through with marriage.

I was done with all sisters. I was done with all women. Pain clouds your judgement. I understand up close and personal the feelings that cause people to make forever decisions in fleeting moments. I know what it is to sit with it. My calculations brought me to, **NOPE**. In its non-verbal state, I had decided: **NEVER AGAIN**.

I reasoned, I'll just be like Jeremiah and Paul. I was going to go on by myself and see what the end was going to be. Beloved, we have all things in common. I was convinced by my circumstances. To reconsider, would take something or someone greater than what happened.

What Did Boaz See?

And Boaz answered and said unto her, It hath fully been shewed me, all that thou hast done unto they mother-in-law since the death of thine husband: and how thou hast left they father and they mother, and the land of thy nativity, and art come unto a people which thou knewest not heretofore.

Ruth 2:11

Boaz saw Ruth serving. Ruth postured (behaved) herself in a way that caused Boaz to take notice. Her character said she had not surrendered to the season. Her attitude and outlook, despite the past, was not one of heaviness.

Man of God, you do not have to expect the negative outcomes of divorce, a painful breakup, or the death of a mate. Woman of God, beyond the shock of what happened is healing and another day. Like Ruth, you can have a healthy posture.

You too can say, "Lord I want to be married again. I believe I want to open my heart again."

There were many women who served before Boaz in his field. It is how you posture yourself that will make the difference. Ruth's posture got Boaz's attention. It was not by accident! All things were working together for Ruth, who loved the Lord. We witness one of her earliest convictions in Ruth 1:16, where she said, "…and thy God, shall be my God."

Ruth chose to glean in the field that belonged to Boaz. While some consider this to be mere coincidence, others believe this was by divine providence. There were plenty of sisters, yet Ruth was the one noticed. She stood out amongst all the rest. She had that umph! Ruth had that flair, that sparkle, that "special something." In the early 80's during my unsaved days of listening to Carl Carlton, she was a "Bad Mama Jamma."

Boaz saw Ruth in the field, but he did not know who she was. She had all the attributes of a virtuous woman recommended in Proverbs 31. Everything he was looking for; he saw it in Ruth. Upon greeting her he said, "Your reputation has preceded you."

It would help you to remember King Lemuel's mother in Proverbs 31, who taught her son what type of woman to look for. Make sure she is a homemaker. Make certain she can "handle her business" and know in and out of the merchant's place. She was a businesswoman. You can be a businesswoman also. You can make six figures, but you must know how to shift and put your CEO title down. When you come into your home, you must put those badges down. As you serve at home, you must be a mother.

You have to take that doctorate degree, or that position on your job and put it on the shelf for the evening. Don't allow your degree to bleed into your weekend. Enjoy the softball game with your daughter. Be present and engaged at the basketball game with your son. You must know how to shift. Your business or your ministry will be okay when you return. You cannot be so deep in your church that you miss ministering to your family.

I am never guilty about the service that I've been called to. When it's time to preach, speak in tongues or prophesy, I dedicate myself to it. I can be everything spiritual and never compare it to being with or assisting my wife. These two things never have to compete.

My gifts are never at risk when I travel to an NBA game. God never takes a back seat when I'm invited to the Bar Association meeting. God is not threatened by basketball nor the law office. I'm learning to be content with the time allocated to the specific purpose. Cooking dinner for my wife and exhorting the body of Christ requires service. I'm called to do both without comparing or neglecting either.

Before She Disclosed Everything

Ruth is a woman whose reputation (character) preceded her. Boaz did not know who she was, but recognized some qualities (attributes, some peculiarities, honorable mannerisms) before he knew who she was. It was before she disclosed "everything" that he noticed her! What is common in this day of social media, some women make known, broadcast, and go public with all the details of their life. They leave nothing to the imagination and diminish the thrill of the chase.

This may be a good time for those of you who are internet dating to change your profile. Your profile should not be filled with so much content. It should be a short characterization (portrayal) of you that does not reveal your whole life.

Unsaved guys used the metaphor, "giving up the cookies" when referring to going all the way or having sexual relations. They pat themselves on the back about their experiences and what a woman was willing to do, too soon. These are men on the streets, bragging about women in the church, some of whom are preachers. Ruth's reputation preceded her, **SO DOES YOURS**.

Fool Me Once...

I will not fall for the same trick. In transparency, I shared with you that my experience being married before left me cynical. Yes, I was a little sour, disappointed, skeptical, and intolerant. I lost the willingness to forbear that kind of intimacy where I would once again be vulnerable enough to hurt. I was done with women. I had gone through enough. As the saying goes, fool me once...

I pray that this message is unlocking the door(s) for you. Man of God, you have not permitted yourself to trust another woman. Woman of God, you are guarded and will not give your heart to another man. I was there. For all the things I endured, I created a necessary haven that turned out later to be a prison. I could not think about moving from that space.

God reached out to me through a brother, who saw what I was going through and who had been praying with me. It is important to emphasize that he had been praying with me. I was not expecting what I would hear next, but I needed it. God had revealed to him that my situation would end up in a divorce before it happened. Then the man of God released these words, "man, you are a good man in ministry." He said, "you deserve the best in your life". He began to describe this virtuous type of woman. He began to describe "my very own Ruth", who I affectionately call **"Grace Girl, Marvel Avenger, my superhero."**

He began to describe the type of woman God was going to bless me with. God was encouraging my heart and letting me know that the relationship that was heading to a divorce would not be a death sentence for me. God was mindful of me and promised to reward me. She would be a woman who carried herself well, one who was well-respected. This man of God was describing the woman who in my estimation would be the whole package. Oblivious to who she was and unaware of what she looked like, wasn't enough to stop me from visiting the church where she attended. I wanted to meet her.

How Are You Doing?

Can you believe it? That was the best I had as I approached her. I introduced myself and she responded by letting me know who she was. I informed her that I had heard or learned about her through someone who spoke well of her. As the conversation continued, I was comfortable to share with her that at that time, due to the recent pain experience in my life, that I just needed a friend. "I don't need anything other than a good friend. I'm in a tough spot." I said, "I would like to get to know you based upon what I've heard about you." To some of you, it was too early to be over-sharing, but I just wanted to be upfront with my intentions.

Audacity has been defined as the willingness to take risks. It can include having the nerve or guts to attempt something that might make you a laughingstock. There she was, looking up at me, shaking her head. In my mind, she was saying, "This man has come in here with this Steve Harvey suit on, looking like an undertaker that's getting ready to embalm someone." Of course, in my mind, I stepped up in the church, clean and "cologned" down. My blessing that day was that I left with the digits. I called her and the rest is history. God divinely hooked it up.

Still Pending

Let me be very clear. God divinely hooked it up. I took the steps to go to meet her after I was divorced from my first marriage. Being legally separated wasn't enough. As long as there was a divorce pending, in the eyes of God I was still married. This will only mean something to those of you who are righteous. God did not nor will He ever authorize you to date someone while you are still legally married. It's as wrong as two left shoes.

This bears repeating: If you are legally separated and the divorce is pending, dating someone is out of the will of God. It doesn't matter if you are being pursued, or if you are doing the pursuing, it is OFF LIMITS while you are still married. You cannot ask God to bless you when you are committing adultery. That's what it is. It's emotional adultery. God will not have you making attachments to someone when a chapter in your life has not been closed. Whenever you begin right, you can continue building on it with confidence. I pray that you receive these instructions that are hard to come by in most religious circles, communities, and churches.

The Value of Instructions

Ruth went back to Naomi. Ruth followed the instructions of her mother-in-law. This was the man, Boaz, and these were his words:

And Boaz answered and said unto her, It hath fully been shewed me, all that thou has done unto they mother-in-law since the death of thine husband and how thou hast left they father and thy mother, and the land of thy nativity, and art come unto a people which thou knowest not heretofore. The Lord recompense thy work, and a full reward be given thee of the Lord God of Israel, under whose wings thou art come to trust.

Ruth 2:11-12

Ruth was trying to process what happened that day. How would she respond to those words from Boaz that comforted her? He spoke friendly to her though she was not like one of his handmaidens. What is the meaning of this? He even allowed her to glean among the sheaves. He was making allowances for Ruth to partake of his produce. There was a portion that he wanted her to have of the barley that remained.

What is the meaning of this, Ruth thought? And she went back and told Naomi of all that had occurred. "His name is Boaz! I have gleaned in his fields today." Suddenly, there was a shift. And Naomi said unto her daughter-in-law, "Blessed be he of the Lord…" It was as though Naomi had gotten a breakthrough in her spirit. This was one of those breakthroughs that you experience after praying for something in secret and God rewards you openly. Naomi witnessed that this was a manifestation of answered prayer.

Naomi needed that breakthrough! She had been grieving the loss of her husband and two sons, one of which was Ruth's husband. Naomi who was known for being pleasant, returned from Moab after these tragedies, bitter. How can any good come from a situation as bad as this? Most of us have been there. Contrary to what some believe, you can be in the grieving process and still believing God for a miracle. Ruth's new information made a difference. The mother-in-law who was once despondent had a glimmer (speck of light) in her eyes. She knew God was about to do something.

Naomi did not have much to offer Ruth by way of expectation, earlier. In her despondency, there wasn't much wisdom to help anyone's situation. How could she advise another when she herself was low in spirit? Beloved, no matter how spiritual or anointed; no matter how well-versed the minister or evangelist, heartbreak is a sideliner. Even with good intentions, until a vessel is healed, they could offer you counsel out of a bitter spirit.

If you can receive this, despondency is a real place. It can manifest in sadness, hopelessness, and defeatism. That individual, no matter how anointed, may not be the best person to advise you.

Psalms 1:1 - Blessed is the man or woman (paraphrased) that does not walk in the counsel of the ungodly. Even a righteous person can give (ungodly) counsel if they are not healed. Though it wouldn't be intentionally to harm, any counsel coming out of their emotions and their damaged soul and not from the Spirit of God will be misleading. Your spirit is what you need vertically to contact God or the things of the spirit. Your soul, however, is what you need to communicate with people horizontally on this earth. When damage has been done to the soul, you cannot give a person accurate counsel.

Ruth went back! She pondered on the meaning of all the events that happened and Boaz's kindness. Naomi would have the answer, she thought. So Ruth sought instruction from her mother-in-law. In doing so, something shifted in Naomi's spirit. She saw a chance to be happy again.

Your well-being still matters to others. It does others good to know that you have the potential for happiness. The idea of you connecting with someone that is compatible with you makes them glad for you.

Could this be, thought Naomi? God is about to reward my daughter-in-law. After seasons of faithfulness, she deserved it. It's her season for redemption. Naomi's perspective changed and so she forgot about herself. She put herself aside for a moment and yielded to the counsel of God. Now she could pour out advice to help Ruth.

Proverbs 15:22 says what? It says without counsel purposes are disappointed, but in the multitude of counsel, they are established.

No Respecter, Sister!

Both Ruth and Orpah were privy to the counsel of Naomi during an inconvenient season. The counsel that was given was from the flesh. Death, struggle, and famine were all around. Naomi was having some mental health issues and could barely motivate herself, let alone the wives of her two sons that had recently passed away.

Momma Naomi was old, too old to consider producing any more sons. It would be better if her daughters-in-law returned to their own people. Maybe they would have some sort of chance to a future. Ruth's sister, Orpah, decided to return to her people. She heeded the counsel of an inconvenient season, "go back to your gods, your mother's house, go back and get you a husband." Orpah went back because she saw the opportunity to go back and get a husband. Ruth, reacted differently, even though she heard the same counsel that helped Orpah make up her mind to return to her own people. Ruth had connected with Naomi. She recognized that her destiny was in this woman's spirit.

Special Delivery

Never put yourself in a position where you're so thirsty for a husband that you are willing to abandon your peaceful place as a single Christian. Don't allow your desire for physical intimacy to motivate you to give up all that God has invested in you. This is not the time nor the place. Some of you are on the potter's wheel. You are being processed for greatness. Don't give up the things of God just to have a man.

This is not the time nor the place for tampering with the anointing of the grace on your life by yielding to corrupt influence, allowing worldly devices to alter your walk and stance with God. It's your birthright. Fight for it. This is the day to dig deep and declare, I'm not going to give up my birthright and my blessing for the sake of sex. Don't sell out to just any partner for the sake of identifying that you have a husband.

The blessing of the Lord, it maketh rich, and he addeth no sorrow with it.

Proverbs 10:22

- Ruth's Confession:
- I'm not willing to lose what God has for me.
- Wherever you go, I'm going to go.
- I'm going to press on.
- I'm going to seek first the kingdom of God and His righteousness.
- I'm going to run on and see what's going to be added to me.
- Where you die, I'm going to die.
- Your God's going to be my God.
- I'm not going to leave God for the sake of a man.

Ruth's confession touched the heart of God. We later see how God providentially arranges for her a husband. God did not send her a thrift store type husband. ...Neither did God send her the "used" type of husband. God sent her a husband right off the showroom floor: a quality husband. Ruth would later be impregnated and gave birth to a son, Obed. Obed would later have a son, called Jesse, the father of Ruth's great-grandson called David.

All this was providentially arranged by the Spirit of God. God saw that Ruth was both steadfastly minded to stay with Naomi and determined to serve her God.

Prostrating Yourself with the Spirit of Abstinence

Abstinence is voluntary, of your own free will. The young woman or the young man who voluntary restrains themself decides not to participate or take part in something. These persons have decided to honor God rather than give in to their desires. They prostrate or position themselves to be subject to a holy life through abstinence until the ordained time to marry.

There are not many mothers! I'm talking about the type of mothers who would sit a young woman down and make eye contact, saying, "In order to get a man, you don't have to show him yourself." You do not have to carry on with a young man in the same manner that a married woman does in matrimony. Your body is not for sampling. As a holy woman of God, you have to prostrate yourself in a state of abstinence. In other words, when you are single, you are to exercise celibacy (NO SEX).

Living holy, may not be popular, but it's right in the sight of God. It's a choice to be kept in a world that is oversexualized.

That He Might Be Glorified

---

*For there is nothing covered, that shall not be
revealed; neither hid, that shall not be known.*

Luke 12:2

For those who have determined to live a life of abstinence,
it's not healthy to sneak and peep around on the internet using
social media as a tool. Like Nicodemus by night, men
occasionally come to my office at work for advice and counsel.
Some of them make it their business to point out women in the
church whose character is suspect; women who are making
connections using social media.

When church girls' private lifestyle doesn't measure up to
their public persona, these men ridicule and brag about how
they conquered them. One such case was regarding an
associate minister. Through internet dating, she met this guy
who pretended to be something he was not. He knew ministry
protocols, church etiquette, and scriptures.

They ended up going out. Before they were even engaged,
they had sexual intercourse.

This young lady was anointed, on the praise team, and
holding a position in the church, one of authority.

The young man showed me on the internet where she
attends church. After the young man left my office, a tear came
fell from my eye. All I could do was take it to God in prayer.
There were moments when I thought to go to her church
service and expose her, but that was the will of flesh as

opposed to what God wanted. Only God can deal with her heart for change to occur.

Give Not Your Strength Unto a Woman

"Give not your strength unto a woman." The new living translation says to a loose woman! In case you didn't know, men like a package that they can look at, but they can't touch, taste or handle.

Other God-fearing brothers and I cover you by encouraging you to, "Pull that dress up, cover your cleavage. You are no stranger to the size of clothes that you should be wearing. You don't have to dress provocative to win a man."

Men, don't give your strength. Don't give your purity to a loose woman. Remember Boaz and how he came to know Ruth. He told her who he was and she gleaned in his field. Boaz blessed her with increase and instructed the young men not to touch her. He was respectful and did not treat her with disrespect. He was concerned with God's purpose for Ruth's life. Sister, this is the type of man that you should be drawn to. When you start dating and become friends, conversations about sex too early ought to present some red flags. Be watchful! No man has a right to come into the life of God's anointed and as early as the third chat on the internet, he asks you about your sexuality. Be watchful! Sharing information about how long you've been without a man, only make you bait for the hook.

Ruth's mother-in-law instructed her on what to do and what not to do. Ruth marked (noticed) the place where Boaz was lying and went in to uncover his feet. At midnight the man was startled, and he turned over, and behold, a woman lay at his feet! And he said, Who are you? And she answered, I am

Ruth your maidservant. Spread your wing [of protection] over your maidservant, for you are a next of kin (Ruth 3:8-9).

Boaz cautioned Ruth, "Don't tell anybody you were here." This righteous man was not only protecting himself, but protecting Ruth also from any nasty rumors that could destroy his and her integrity. A righteous man will protect his anointing. Simultaneously, he will not cause you to miss your birthright, forfeit your blessing, discredit your spiritual legacy, or lose your mantle over an occasion to the flesh. Ruth returned home. There was no discredit to either of them. This is the type of woman Lemuel's mother spoke of in Proverbs 31.

Boaz, being older than Ruth, charged the younger men not to touch (molest) her (Ruth 2:9). For some, the idea of God connecting you with someone with an age difference can be intimidating. While age can be a factor, your primary concern should be, does he have the maturity level to build spiritual, mental, physical intimacy? Is this someone who you can connect with intellectually?

Spirit of God, I bless you for this platform. I bless you for allowing your people to trust this vessel. For your word has declared that the earnest expectation of the creature is waiting for the manifestation of the sons of God. Father, I believe that by thy spirit, as the platform has been given, I have deposited by your command, by your leading, by your unction into the spirit of men and women to help them, to produce breakthroughs.

AND I COMMAND A BREAKTHROUGH. *I command a breakthrough to come in your spirit* *right now. I release the anointing of the Holy Ghost. I command the burdens to be removed. I command the yoke to be broken, to be corrected. I command your freedom right now.*

*In Jesus' name. **Hallelujah!!!***

Nurturing the Four Types of Intimacy

Intimacy is not something that is done well inside, nor outside of the church. One reason being, those in relationships see intimacy as being physical only. For this reason, relationships have significantly suffered. Acknowledging physical intimacy alone is like expecting a structure to be held up by one pillar, when there are three other pillars that support and prop up the building. The four types of intimacy in marriage are emotional intimacy, physical intimacy, mental intimacy, and spiritual intimacy. The structure, or the framework of the marriage is held together by agape love, which consists of four posts, instead of one.

Genesis 1:26 – "And God said, let us make man in our image and after our likeness." Verse 27, follows up with "God, so created he, man in his image and in the image of God created him, male and female created he them."

- When God created Adam and Eve, he invested in them these four types of intimacy.

*And God caused a deep sleep to fall upon Adam,
and he slept: and he took one of his ribs, closed
up the flesh instead thereof; and the rib, which
the Lord had taken from man, made he a woman
and brought her unto the man. And Adam said,
This is now bone of my bones, and flesh of my
flesh: she shall be called Woman, because she
was taken out of Man. Therefore shall a man
leave his father and mother, and shall cleave
unto his wife: and they shall be one flesh.*

Genesis 2:21-24

- It was all a part of the framework. Even as God began to mold them, He was connecting them spiritually. Adam and Eve would know one another. God would fasten and link them emotionally, mentally, and physically. God bonded them.

  We see this same set up in St. Matthew 19, verses 4 through 6 - And he answered and said unto them, "Have God made them male and female? And said, For this cause shall a man leave father and mother, and shall cleave to his wife: and they twain shall be one flesh? Wherefore they are no more twain, but one flesh. What therefore God hath joined together, let no man put asunder."

- God amazingly fastened them together. ... And let no man unhitch them.

A Rocky Start

So few people are willing to admit that their marriage got off to a rocky start. We wanted to experience something we couldn't define. Some confused intimacy with some spontaneous, feel-good, sensation.

How would you complete this thought? At the beginning of my marriage, the level of emotional intimacy was:

A. Strong

B. Intense

C. Lacking (came up short)

D. Fierce

E. Empty

Looking back over your marriage, what was the level of emotional intimacy? How was the mental intimacy in the beginning? How was the physical intimacy? At the start of your marriage, what was the level of your spiritual intimacy? Some of the challenges or the way you responded to the challenges can easily be traced back to how you started.

When the foundation or the starting point of the relationship is flawed or faulty the marriage suffers. When the couple begins to have physical relations with one another before they say, "I DO", they have already started the foundation off wrong.

The origin of the word intimacy is derived from the Latin word "intimus", meaning inner or innermost. To have access to, to comprehend his or her innermost character, it means to make familiar. Beloved, the intimacy in a marriage starts off with a friendship. This is rare, as most people, in this day and time, enter engagements too quickly.

As I recommended before, it would be unwise to introduce the person you were recently engaged to, to your family member who cannot make proper judgement. Rather, I encourage you to bring them before spiritual authority instead of family. Sometimes parents don't have to be born again to assist in this area. God gives parents instinct to know if someone is right or wrong for you. Acknowledge them with their concerns and believe that what they're saying is best for you. Now if you have a parent that just can't discern, don't have perception, or doesn't have insight, you may need to go to your pastor. If not your parent(s), take them before your aunt. If not a guardian, allow someone who is able to consider, weigh in and assess certain characteristics by examining your potential mate.

One of the things I learned from Apostle Donald Fozard, who I was ordained under, is you must always inspect what you expect. You must allow someone to inspect the person that you're going to invite into your life, that you want to become one with.

One of the enemies that block real intimacy in marriage is keeping secrets. Self-disclosure has proven to be healthy in a relationship. On the contrary, refusing to disclose personal details about yourself can hinder connections. Vulnerability exists when you can share your past, things that you have been through, and things that were done to you with the person you are connecting with. Being vulnerable can be challenging. Refusing to disclose information can prevent you from developing a meaningful bond with your potential mate.

You must be willing to open your heart from the beginning so that those 4 pillars of intimacy: emotional, spiritual, mental and physical can be instituted.

The word of the Lord says, "Be not unequally yoked together with unbelievers." Beloved, please don't make the mistake of connecting with somebody that is not born again. If you connect with somebody that is not born again and you marry that person, you will miss out on the type of spiritual intimacy that God intended. God intended for you and your spouse to be likeminded. God's idea for your relationship was that both of you would walk in agreement. God purposed that both of you, together, would handle challenges with the truth of the Word of God. It was and still is God's idea that husbands and wives, worship together.

When the couple is unequally yoked, either the husband or the wife is saved while the other one is unsaved. Here we have two different natures, one that is like God and the other, unlike God.

Invitation to Trouble

He desires fellowship. She desires fellowship. "…but what fellowship have the righteous with unrighteousness? What communion of darkness of life have he not believed with an infidel? Now you have an uninvited guest: TROUBLE! "Come out from among them. Be separated. Touch not the unclean thing." God gives clear instructions to the believers to help us avoid unnecessary pitfalls and bondages. Mistakes are costly! Don't allow yourself to be motivated by the pressures of getting old. People are pushing (influencing) you by reminding you of your desire to have children. Not to mention that so many are in love with the idea of being married that they ignore all the red flags.

A Space Reserved for My Mate

Beloved, I caution you, do not open your heart to anyone in a greater capacity than you do to your spouse. No one should have your heart or your ear greater than your spouse. Emotional intimacy is damaging, it drains your marriage when you share your heart and give your ear to someone else more than to your spouse. Don't give that space to anyone else other than your mate. These were the wise words I received when interviewing a wise man of God who attends the same fellowship as I. He and his wife have a beautiful marriage that has lasted over 35 years.

It is not wise for a wife to disclose personal problems existing with her husband to another man.

Men, when you are going through, don't disclose your information to a single woman, or one who is experiencing a failing marriage, as she can't give you any advice if she's having challenges herself. However, if she is married and healed, a ministry gift or a wise woman, that's different.

Being vulnerable is easier for some than others. You are opening and exposing yourself to someone who you perceive to be safe. You are not opening yourself up to be attacked nor to be an easy target. No one can digest your entire past over dinner. Ask the Holy Spirit to teach you how to share gradually. This is the person that you are inviting into your life. Getting to know them includes some of the details, specific experiences, contacts, and encounters that helped shape them. Don't shy away from background checks. Go ahead, ask them!!!

You are sharing your heart. You are developing a level of intimacy with someone you are about to be married to. The bond that you're creating will support and remind you that your partner is a safe place. When times of testing come in the relationship, the enemy can't use fear and mistrust to cause you to withdraw from your mate and seek out the listening ear of another.

Sharing yourself, sharing your heart and giving your ear to other people, can end in disaster.

Like Eve, many of you consider it to be harmless. In Genesis the third chapter we see how this very thing messed up Adam's and Eve's spiritual intimacy. When Eve gave her ear, the serpent began to tell Eve things that were different than what God said and contrary to how God directed her and Adam as a married couple.

What happened to what God instructed to guide them? The moment she gave her ear to the serpent, the moment he suggested that it was in her favor to eat of the tree, in that instant, she should have sought out Adam.

Before Eve took of the fruit, she should have gone back to (turned to, sought the advice of, or consulted with) her covering.

 Adam, There is a Serpent in the Garden...

This is what Eve should have done. Adam, something is bothering me. Remember when God told us ... "But of the tree of knowledge of good and evil, thou shalt not eat of it: for in the day that thou eat thereof thou shalt surely die." Well, how about the serpent said to me today, that the in the day we eat thereof, our eyes will be opened, and we shall be as gods, knowing good and evil. I let him know that God told us not to even touch it. Then all of a sudden, my eyes fastened on that tree and I shook my head and ran home as fast as I could. Adam, I need your help. I felt myself getting weak. Can you remind me of what God said?

This is what Eve could have done, but she didn't. She gave her ear. She opened up herself emotionally. She was challenged in the area of spiritual intimacy and emotional intimacy as well. These challenges affected the foundation of their marriage. I pray that God will help you and others that you know, break the habit of emptying out all your trash, venting, broadcasting your business to the first person willing to listen. Any and every one, no matter how kind, can't handle the weight of what you're dealing with. Seek out your pastor or his counseling team for assistance. Don't be afraid to make decisions that are best for you. You may need someone who is certified to speak in the specific area that you need help. If they are not qualified, shut it down and put the counseling session on hold.

Physical Intimacy

In the mind of many, when defining intimacy, they immediately think about that which is done with the body. Physical intimacy, referring to body closeness, is what people relate to the most. It is the connection that is experienced when hugging, cuddling, kissing, and holding hands. Physical intimacy is about sexual intercourse, and what people do with their bodies. The Bible makes known God's will in the area of physical intimacy. It is a need in marriage. Husbands and wives are to give their consent (agreement), to be physically affectionate toward one another.

Let the husband render unto the wife due benevolence: and likewise also the wife unto the husband.

I Corinthians 7:3

The word of the Lord goes on to say in verse 5, "Defraud not one another." No matter how mad you get with your mate, you are in error, and you are working emotional witchcraft, and you are emotionally abusing your mate when you withhold to try to control him or her. Yes, I said it! It's in the word of God. "…Satan tempts you when you refuse to give physical intimacy or have sexual intercourse with your mate because you're mad, angry, and upset! Because he or she can't go to anyone other than you, this refusal is opening the door for physical adultery to occur in your marriage.

Physical adultery begins with emotional adultery. Your spouse begins to think about someone else, all because you've decided that you're going to control them by withholding that which you agreed to before a righteous God.

Emotional Intimacy

Emotional intimacy is healthy. It is about being close to another with your feelings and reactions. It's okay to be emotional and not be an emotional wreck. It includes being transparent with your deepest feelings, your fears, your thoughts. By the way, we all have feelings. Acknowledging them doesn't make you weak nor a pushover. Learning how to express and manage them when it matters will help you in your marriage relationship.

It should not take you forever to get to know someone. You need to know what you are getting into before making a commitment. How does the person sitting across the table respond emotionally? What kinds of things about themselves have they disclosed that help you understand them better? If you are going to invest in this relationship, you must know if you have the capacity to ride with them. His or her emotional state may prove to be overwhelming, but honesty upfront will let you know if you want to invest. I don't recommend pouring yourself out, disclosing all your emotions at once. There are some things that need to be reserved until after the engagement. Don't let your love of the idea of being married prematurely open up too much of yourself to someone who is unqualified. Reject the idea of having to share the compartments of your heart with a stranger. Emotional intimacy has to be managed. If not properly managed a couple can find themselves having sexual intercourse before saying, "I DO"!

Eye Gates...

In order to get a better perspective and understanding of women, I've had the privilege of dialoging with a couple of women ministers. They shared two things that are happening in the church that are hardly ever talked about. Some men in the church, and even some who confess Christ as Lord and Savior, are struggling with pornography.

When something or someone presents themselves to you in a seductive way, you have to immediately cast it down or turn away. Smiling at the gesture is not an option. This would be one of those times when the skill of managing your emotions would benefit. It just so happens that they said something flattering. It was just the attention you needed since your husband hadn't told you that he loved you the entire week. I encourage you, rather than entertaining it, unmask it and pull back the curtain. Make it known unto your mate.

When something comes across your desk, that is not of God, you must expose it. Some random woman thinking I was her boyfriend, inadvertently sent me a nude picture one night when I was at work. She persisted in sending two or three more. I could have decided, "Oh, (in a surprising manner) her body looks attractive." I could have responded back to her. I could have.

Because I love my wife and our marriage, I wanted to keep that door shut. The enemy thought to access my marriage by sending me pornographic pictures. I showed my wife the nude pictures. I said: "Look what the devil had the audacity to send me, some nude pictures of this woman, thinking that I'm her boyfriend". My wife asked me, "Why are you showing me this?" I replied, "I don't want to be sitting around thinking about nobody else or being involved with anyone other than you. Satan thought to plant the seed of adultery through the eye gates.

It was the same type scenario that David encountered after seeing Bathsheba. The reason he wanted Bathsheba is because he saw her. (II Samuel 11: 2). He saw her with no clothes on. She was very beautiful to behold. Her nudity influenced him to inquire about her identity. He would have not even thought about committing adultery, but he saw her and eventually took her.

When stuff like that tries to get to your eye gates or your ear gates, you have to cast it down and you have to be willing to expose it to your mate. My wife and I practice this in our marriage. Whenever either of us are approached by someone else, we expose the strategies of the enemy. On occasions when inappropriate looks come from single or married women, I share it with my wife. If you value your marriage, this is what you have to do. Keep the doors shut! Don't invite it. Don't return it back. …And do not shelter it from your mate.

How Do I Know If My Mate and I Have Emotional Intimacy?

Where is the evidence? Where is the testimony that supports emotional intimacy in my marriage? Emotional intimacy is validated when someone is continually involved in your life other than yourself. The evidence is you willing to open up. Your testimony is the rewards you are experiencing in being vulnerable to your mate.

There is a big difference between being vulnerable with your mate and the man or woman you just met on the internet. The person you are dating online can't provide the proper comfort for you. You're pouring out your heart, while they are asking you detailed questions regarding personal matters. REJECT, the interview. Don't give them too much information too soon.

Set Your Boundaries

There must be an emotional barrier that is exclusively for your husband. Likewise, there has to be an emotional barrier that is exclusively for your wife. Keep other men and women out!

Your silence is compliance. Keep the doors closed. My wife responds to compliments by replying, "My husband tells me that too." Be ready to combat what the enemy is trying to create, even if you are going through. Imaginations will try and come. Your feelings may get intrigued. Someone noticed you. Be ready to combat and cast down imaginations. Jesus said something; "It is written" (Matthew 4). You have to say something also.

Sticking together, joining, allegiance, and prioritizing affections can all be summed up by **EMOTIONAL INTIMACY**. Genesis 2:24 says it this way, "Therefore shall a man leave his father and his mother, and shall cleave unto his wife. And while it sounds nice, it has proven to be a thorn in the flesh of your mate's flesh. They've sought the Lord about it more than thrice and yet their in-laws keep showing up with unwanted suggestions about how to run the marriage. Beloved, it is vital that you leave and cleave! There is a level of emotional intimacy that is long awaiting your marriage as soon as your parents stop interfering when the scent of something is going wrong. In-laws are not supposed to run your marriage!!!

Every time something goes wrong, your first reaction is to run back home. How can we ever test the glue if you keep jumping ship and going over and staying the night? They've only heard your version of what happened and yet they are offering what you should do. This is not the prescription for a healthy relationship.

Word from the Lord (WFTL):

The Lord said to tell you, when you and your husband are troubleshooting you have to get a handle on your emotions. When you are working through the problem you have to have empathy for your mate. Somehow you have to recognize the person sitting across from you and have an understand that they are trying to repair what's broken. Conflict resolution suggests that you are at least willing to confront the disagreement and attempt to reconcile. Wives, the Lord is saying, make way for wisdom. Lowering the tone of your voice will assist in restoring the harmony while you are working through the hard stuff. Sometimes men are threatened. Sometimes men feel intimidated when you raise your voice toward them.

But let it be the hidden man of the heart, in that which is not corruptible, even the ornament of a meek and quiet spirit, which is in the sight of God, of great price.

I Peter 3:4

When the Bible speaks of a submissive, high-value, woman, her character is one of a meek and quiet spirit. She is neither clamorous, rowdy nor disorderly. Her demeanor is closely associated with self-discipline, moderation, and restraint. She is intentional in seeking out the best way to handle things without jumping to conclusions. Hardly will she ever provoke another to wrath.

Thank God for my high-value wife, who in the sight of God and I, is of a great price. Her quiet spirit is a delight to me. She seldom raises her voice. And I learned that from her, that when you don't raise your voice and get all clamorous, you can be in control of your emotions just by not getting loud.

Remember, emotional intimacy is an experience for those who are willing to connect. It requires some level of disconnecting from all the things that caused you to be guarded. Some of you have made vows that you will never allow anyone to get close to you again. Those vows will have to be renounced. It's okay to be careful. There's no shame in being reserved with someone you barely know. However, when the time comes, and you meet the right one, moderate disclosure must be part of the engagement.

Mental Intimacy

Just give me someone who I can relate to! It's good to be in the company of someone who gets you. Oh, the reward of having a good rapport with a mate! It's nice to finally have someone who you can share your ideas, opinions, and your life perspectives with. Mental intimacy may also involve intellectually challenging each other.

When you have a certain intellectual level, you should seek to interact with someone whose intellectual level is comparable. To go down on someone else's level requires you to change. The way you communicate and think must adapt to the person who you are getting to know.

Connecting mentally does matter. You want to indulge in meaningful conversations. When the conversations are mutually stimulating it's easier to connect, be in sync with and relate to. Her dialogue should enrich him, as his dialogue should provoke her to engage and share on a deeper level. Choosing someone who isn't intellectually challenging can cause you to later become resentful, impatient, snide (critical), and even bored.

Don't make the mistake of connecting with someone physically, thinking that having sex is enough. Don't be convinced that the new guy in church, with the fresh anointing on his life will completely satisfy you. Then there is the deception that because he makes a lot of money, he checks off everything on your list. If your ideal guy doesn't intellectually challenge you, it could be that you know more than he knows. Sooner or later, you're going to start treating him like your son.

REAL wives desire their Adam to be the head. Real wives want a man to lead with confidence and consistence. Women are reluctant when they are put in a position where they must train and teach men. This has been a hindrance to many relationships. Challenging one another and learning from each other is the preferred scenario.

Some women have more knowledge or are more skill in certain areas than their husbands. Rude is never an excuse to interrupt him. What is it that causes a woman to correct a man whenever he begins to talk. A superior complex will cause you to have an exaggerated point of view. He doesn't need you to overemphasize what you think by overriding what he just said.

Ladies, trying to one-up your husband may be a sign of your inner struggles. No situation is so demanding that you must add your opinion to what he said. This is especially true when you are in a group setting. When in the presence of your parents, instead of trying to challenge him be respectful.

Don't undermine your husband by speaking out of season! Marriage suffers when the things brought to the table by one are constantly being rejected by another. Your constant belittling is damaging to the mental health of the other person. Instead of edifying and building up the person you are relating to, your actions make them seem unimportant.

Who Would Have Thought...

There are certain things that I can't make up, even if I tried. A couple made attempts at developing intellectual and mental intimacy. It's okay to take another look at the narrative just introduced. These areas are among those within a relationship that need to be worked on. Like so many others, the couple's intimacy was being hindered. Something was interfering with what they were trying to achieve. They had no idea, until a moment of complete honesty. It was JEALOUSY.

Jealousy causes you to be competitive with your husband or your wife. Your husband or your wife can be great in certain areas. They may be recognized in certain spiritual circles. They may be a decorated veteran or highly sought after in their business profession. Whatever the accolade, privilege, or esteem, don't get jealous of your mate.

We don't compare ourselves nor measure ourselves. It would be unwise for husbands to compete with their wives. In similar fashion, it would be unwise for wives to compete with their husbands.

If you hear your wife's name called in honor or if you hear your husband's name called in honor, say "Praise God." Always see your mate as an asset and not a competitor. I'm going to say that again. Always see your mate as an asset, adding to your life and not a competitor. Men or women, you don't need to make a fool out of yourself to try to compete with your mate. See them, honor them, praise them. Praise God. It's all in the same pot. It's all in the same household. Praise the name of the Lord. Hallelujah. Never make your mate feel like they must compete against you.

Unwilling to Live in the Shadow of Her Ex

At some point you should begin to prioritize the need to nurture and strengthen mental intimacy in your relationship. Your mate cannot and should not bear the burden of living in someone's shadow. He is not your past husband or your past boyfriend. What they did while you were with them should not cast a shadow over what your mate is doing now, that is new, but unfamiliar.

If you were in a relationship for a length of time as I was, you must be careful with what and how you communicate. After being married for 17 years, I had to catch myself from expecting according to the standards set in a season that was passed. The person I was now with was totally different and deserved to introduce me to a whole range of new things for a new season.

A Person Who Has Stopped Learning Has Stop Growing

Those who debate with their mate place themselves on opposing sides. Rather than competing, I recommend that you choose to learn from one another. While jealousy may be expected by a one believed to be a rival, any enjoyment of advantage experienced by a husband or wife is to share with their spouse.

Iron sharpeneth iron; So a man sharpeneth the countenance of his friend.

Proverbs 27:17

Two are better than one; because they have a good reward for their labour.

Ecclesiastes 4:9

Two incomes are better than one. Two mindsets, two skillsets are better than one. What you can't see, she can see. What you don't discern, he can perceive, comprehend, and understand clearly.

It was Pilate's wife, not Pilate who sat on the throne, who suggested "Touch not this just man, for I have suffered many things in a dream because of him. She sent word to Pilate. When Pilate saw that he could not prevail against the tumult, he released Barabbas into the multitude. The soldiers of the governor took Jesus unto the common hall where they stripped him and put on a scarlet robe. Pilate had yielded to the crowd to crucify Jesus and not Barabbas. Pilate was not open to his mate's influence (St. Matthew 27:19-26).

What a lesson it is to learn. Pilate could have benefited from his wife. We too can benefit from our mate's ideas, suggestions, even at the risk of correcting us away from a small or gigantic mistake.

In Steps Abraham...

Abraham had a situation. He slept with the bondwoman. Hagar behavior is now creating tension around the house. Sarah said, "that woman has got to get out of here." Sarah is provoked and cannot bear the day-to-day disregard and lack of respect. No one was prepared to deal with Sarah, a woman damaged emotionally and mentally.

In steps Abraham, and he isn't ready. Abraham, because his emotions were all in the way, he acted as if he wasn't going to put Hagar out. But God, heavenly intelligence, began to download into Abraham, "Do what Sarah said. You must let her go". Abraham had a child by her. He was emotionally connected to her in certain ways, but he had to do what God told him to do.

Abraham connected with Hagar emotionally. This emotional connection affected his relationship with Sarah. You must make sure that you burn all those emotional and mental bridges that you have with other people from the past. You can't keep celebrating, commemorating, and honoring the good times with a person from your past. Refrain from sending happy birthday, Merry Christmas, and happy Mother's Day texts. The scriptures declare, "Your latter will be greater than your former."

Spiritual Intimacy

Spiritual intimacy means feeling close to one another spiritually. She has a relationship with Christ. He has his own relationship with Christ. Now, two born again believers are coming together in relationship together. Their shared relationship with Jesus Christ and their experience with Him, is the foundation that will make a difference. It's who they know that will help them to unite.

Spiritual intimacy develops in a marriage, in a relationship, when both people go for what they know in seeking after God. David says, "As the deer pants after the water, my soul searches after you" (Psalms 42:1). Each person, the husband, and the wife must strive individually. The Bible says in Philippians 2:12, it says, "Work out your own salvation with fear and trembling." Each person must nourish their own, personal, spiritual relationship with God to give to one another.

*Wherefore, my beloved, as ye have always
obeyed, not as in my presence only, but now
much more in my absence, work out your own
salvation with fear and trembling. For it is God
which worketh in you both to will and to do of
his good pleasure.*

Philippians 2:12-13

Not as in my presence

"As ye have obeyed, not as in my presence." How often
are we motivated by the presence of others? That motivation
often wears off when the person(s) is no longer around. Paul
exhorts:

- Not just in the presence of your husband or wife
- Not just when you attend church, in the presence of
  other believers.

Each person must have their individual relationship with
God to pour into one another. Each one must have a prayer life.
Both individuals have to have their own study life. We don't
have to wait for the company of others to obey God. God
inspired my wife a year ago, and as a result we now have
family devotion. She and I and our two seventeen-year-olds sit
around the table and break bread.

It's a blessing to come home and find Jesus as I walk
through the door. The atmosphere is charged with God's
presence as my wife has already entered worship of her own

volition. It's a blessing to step into that type of atmosphere, where it's suitable to bring stuff onto the table spiritually to your mate.

There are some easy conversations to be had which come with little resistance. There are other conversations that require careful consideration, requiring the input of both spouses. The consequence of the household decision lays in the hands of two people who agree or disagree. It helps when each of them is spiritually-minded. One of the consequences of marrying someone who is not saved, or on a lesser spiritual level, is disharmony, lack of understanding and unwillingness to bend. So much for that atmosphere charged with the presence of God… You could arrive home to a frustrated, burned-out spouse who is tired of being pushed around and taken for granted.

Suddenly you seem to remember the counselor repeatedly emphasizing how the timing of God mattered when getting married. Now you see the significance of marrying someone who is compatible with your spiritual development. If you have been saved for 20 to 30 years, and you marry a person who is spiritually younger, you can't expect them to be as God conscience as you are. In other words, they will perceive what God justifies or approves of differently than you. You are going to have some challenges.

Understanding the Difference

There Is a Difference!
Romans chapter 8 speaks about how a carnal minded person is enmity against God. It speaks to Christians under development. Paul speaks of the creature that waiteth for the

manifestation of the sons of God. These sons of God are being challenged to identify with God. In identifying, they are still being processed in some areas.

And I, brethren, could not speak unto you as unto spiritual, but as unto carnal, even as unto babes in Christ. I have fed you with milk, and not with meat: for hitherto ye were not able to bear it, neither yet now are ye able. For ye are yet carnal: for whereas there is among you envying, and strife, and divisions, are ye not carnal, and walk as men?

1 Corinthians 3:1-3

There is yet evil in you! There is still jealousy and other fleshly works in your life. Paul addressed them because of their carnality of not laying aside certain things. You have determined that you are ready. As much as you want us to believe that your potential mate is ready, some part of you has probably not discerned nor assessed the situation. He's handsome but wait. He's bow-legged but **DO NOT** yield. He has plenty of the money you have prayed for God to send, but it will end up costing you, if you leap. He served 20 years faithfully in the church but has no relationship with God. You must weigh all those facts when deciding to wait or move ahead. Whatever you decide will determine your level of spiritual intimacy in your marriage.

Consequences

A. The frustration of trying to beg your mate to come to church.
B. The emptiness of desiring your spouse to seek God in prayer to no avail.
C. The lengthy debates over "paying" tithes.

All these things and more... These are the things you need to factor in before you say, "I do". Before you get engaged and pour all your heart out, weigh out these matters. It's best to do it now, before you get engaged and later regret your decision.

This is what God says about it: (Galatians 6:7-8) "As a man soweth, that shall he also reap." If you enter a relationship prematurely, you bring consequences to your mate. You bring consequences on yourself.

"Trust takes years to build, seconds or minutes to break, and forever to repair."

Dhar Mann

- Where trust has been violated, make sure that you demand to your mate that trust be repaired.
- You can't build a foundation where trust is not at the center.
- When trust has been violated, it must be repaired properly to begin to build on it.
- The person who breaks and violates the covenant must be held accountable.

Sex Is Not a Number

But The King "Knew" Her Not

But the King (did not have sex) was not intimate with her

Now, King David was old and stricken in years; and they covered him with clothes, but he gat no heat. Wherefore his servants said unto him, Let there be sought for my lord the king a young virgin; and let her stand before the king, and let her cherish him, and let her lie in thy bosom, that my lord the king may get heat. So they sought for a fair damsel throughout all the coast of Israel and found Abishag, a Shunammite, and brought her to the king. And the damsel was very fair, and cherished the king, and ministered unto him, but the king knew her not.

I Kings 1:1-4

After I Am Waxed Old, Shall I Have Pleasure

...And She LAUGHED!

---

*Therefore Sarah laughed within herself saying,
After I am waxed old shall I have pleasure, my
Lord being old also? And the Lord said unto
Abraham, Wherefore did Sarah laugh, saying,
Shall I of a surety bear a child, which am
old? Is anything too hard for the Lord? At the
time appointed, I will return into thee according
to the time of life, and Sarah shall have a son,*

Genesis 18:12-14

---

*As it is written, I have made thee a father of
many nations before him whom he believed,
even God, who quickeneth the dead, and calleth
those things that be not as though they were.
Who against hope believed in hope, that he
might become the father of many nations,
according to that which was spoken, So shall
thy seed be. And being not weak in faith, he
considered not his own body, now dead, when
he was about hundred years old, neither yet the
deadness of Sarah's womb: He staggered not at
the promises of God through unbelief, but was
strong in faith, giving glory to God; And being
fully persuaded that what he had promised, he
was able also to perform.*

Romans 4:17-21

People age! We age! The scriptures above help us to navigate a process that many, even born-again believers struggle with. No matter how much we try to ignore it, we all are coming to that day when our bodies will not do, will not have the capacity we had when we were younger. There is no exception with King David. In I Kings, he is an older man (stricken in years), who is known for fancying himself with different wives and female companionship.

King David is suffering with a condition called hypothermia. It is a potentially dangerous condition due to abnormal low body temperature. And his servants recommended a young fair virgin be sought out to stand before him, cherish him, lie in his bosom that he may get heat.

Throughout all the coast they sought and brought him a fair damsel who ministered unto him. ... But the king knew her not (vs. 4). In his old age, King David, could not perform. There was no fulfillment. Despite the good intentions of his servants, the king could not get any heat. And beloved, as we get older in age, our bodies sometimes can't perform the way that they did before.

There are several factors that may contribute. It may be different for some than others. This is not an exhaustive list but just to name a few:

- Erectile Dysfunction
- HSDD (Hypoactive Sexual Desire Disorder)
- Perimenopause / Postmenopause

When these things come, we have to make adjustments. You can do it! You made adjustments when financial challenges hit your marriage. You made adjustments when you encountered health challenges. You've done it before. Some of you had to adjust when you decided to marry into a ready-made family. Chances are, your original idea of being married didn't include someone that had children already. Some adjustments are small changes while others take considerable time. Depending on your new in-laws, it could go either way. Just as you've done before, you can make the necessary adjustment, even when it comes to a decline in your normal sexual performance.

Support Your Mate During Unexpected Decline

No one was waiting around for this to happen! No one was expecting this today. However disappointing this could be to the person(s) in the marriage, making your spouse feel bad is not the answer. This is not the time to make your husband feel like he's less of a man or your wife like she's less of a woman.

In preparing for a time of intimacy, a woman may set the mode, by choosing certain attire that makes her comfortable and captivates her husband. They planned a romantic get-away at the beach, ocean-front property. The wind just so happens to be blowing just right. It's the perfect evening, nothing could go wrong. The only thing wrong is he can't perform. This is an unfortunate situation for him; one he didn't ask for. Don't beat him up with words. The situation calls for you to make adjustments.

When a woman occasionally suffers with Hypoactive Sexual Disorder (HSDD), or when women go through the periods of post menopause and perimenopause, when they just don't feel up to it, husbands have to adjust. Making the necessary adjustment is easier when we dwell (live considerately) with our wives according to knowledge. The changes in their physical bodies present real challenges.

- BUILD upon emotional intimacy.
- BUILD upon mental intimacy.
- BUILD upon spiritual intimacy.

As you age, it is important to build. It is important that you are building and balancing the four types of intimacy in your marriages. If the time come when there is a decline in your physical normal ability to have sexual relations, then you will still have something to rest upon.

As I began to seek the face of God, the Father began to say, "That's why people develop the desire to jump out of marriages." Some women justify their desire to leave when the man can't perform as usual. When a woman loses interest in intercourse as a result of physical changes in her body, some men see it as a pass to jump out of the marriage. Neither of the reasons mentioned gives the wife nor the husband a pass.

When a husband or a wife entertains thoughts like "since you aren't doing enough, I'm justified in engaging in porn and finding ways to fulfill my own sexual needs." Some disregard the part of the vows that say, "for better or worse." Instead, they seek out what appears to be greener pastures, step outside of their marriage and end up suffering.

They had no idea of the dangers lurking in what appeared to be greener grass. They weren't aware that there might be a cobra or a scorpion waiting to prey upon those who opened the door for adultery. This can be extremely devastating for children. Adultery now controls the environment that their children have to grow up in.

Low Libido Doesn't Have to be a Liability

Along with David's suffering with the condition of hypothermia, he was not able to perform. David was experiencing low libido. He was experiencing what is common upon men of a certain age, erectile dysfunction, inability of a man to maintain an erection sufficient enough for sexual pleasure.

It is a lack of blood flow just like David had a lack of body heat that prevented him from performing once he got older. When they put the Shunammite (beautiful young virgin) in his bosom, he could not perform because his body temperature was too low. At that time, David was what we call impotent. He was not able to perform.

As you mature in age and your husband gets older, he may suffer from impotence. Some women have said, "I'm out of here, and he can't do anything for me". You don't have the right to jump ship. Impotence is a chronic inability to obtain or sustain an erection for the performance of a sexual act. Educate yourself about this very real challenge that's rarely talked about in the church. This is common to man. – I Corinthians 10:13.

Low libido, doesn't have to be a liability. The scripture goes on to say, …that you are able to bear." God will not put more on you nor suffer you to be tempted above that you are able. There are other factors that accompany low libido that makes this a difficult time for men. Thank God for his promise of making a way of escape that men can bear and endure when this season occurs.

Do it! Obey God! Rise up in the name of Jesus and escape, by strengthening the mental intimacy in your marriage. It's okay to receive the answers you have been waiting for. God wants us to strengthen the spiritual intimacy in your marriage, strengthen the emotional intimacy, and the physical intimacy in our marriage which includes hugging, kissing, holding hands, etc.

You Can't Forget the Four Principles

(Emotional, Intellectual, Physical and Spiritual Intimacy)

Marriage stands upon the foundation of these four principles. And Jesus said it in Matthew 7:24, I liken him unto a wise man, which built his house upon a rock. 25 – And the rain descended, and the floods came, and the winds blew, and beat upon that house; and it fell not: for it was founded upon a rock.

When there's a decline in one area of intimacy, because you are continually strengthening other areas of intimacy, then your marriage won't go bankrupt. If you marry someone who is younger in the Lord, grace and patience has to be present until your mate is strengthened in that area. This is only necessary if you desire to have a healthy, spiritual connection. Likewise, the same is necessary when there exist imbalances in other areas of the marriage relationship.

It is said that other areas of the physical body are enhanced when the eyesight or the hearing suffers. The heightened sensitivities of well-known gifts like Stevie Wonder, Ray Charles and even Beethoven are evidence of the body compensating when adjustments are necessary.

Feeling Like the "Only" One Leads to Anxiety

And Elijah said, while on the run from Jezebel, "I'm the only one" and they seek by life to destroy it. (I Kings 1:18, 19). When Jezebel had given threats to kill Elijah, God responded to his anxiety saying, "I have left 7,000 that have not vowed. God rebuked the prophet Elijah. You're not the only one going through it. How common is it for people to suffer in these particular areas, thinking that they are the only one.

Erectile dysfunctions can occur at different ages.

- There are cases where men in their 30s and late 20s are beginning to have challenges.
- Series of test, have revealed that 40% of men in their 40s have a chance of experiencing erectile dysfunction
- At 50, 50% of men have this challenge. Every decade it increases by 10%.
- At age 60, 60% of men have this challenge.
- Testing and analysts reveal that 70% of men at the age of 70 have erectile dysfunction, suffering with some level of impotency.

The ages of impotency vary. Other than age, there are different factors that contribute to its cause. While some men lose their inability to perform at a certain age, others go on to enjoy intimacy with their partner well into their older years.

Shall I Have Pleasure?

Sarah laughed and maybe she was a bit cynical, but the idea of "pleasure" had always been her desire towards Abraham. "Shall I have pleasure" was Sarah's response after hearing God tell Abraham that he and Sarah were going to conceive a child. Pleasure, at my old age? Sarah could not conceive a child. She had reached an age/season when her physical body naturally declines in reproductive hormones. Sarah had experienced menopause.

Twelve months after a woman's menstrual periods permanently cease, her ovaries stop producing reproductive hormones. Along with this comes different physical, mental and emotional challenges. Some suffer with hypoactive sexual disorder during this season of menopause. Hypoactive sexual disorder (HSDD), is characterized by lack of intimacy, as a result of low sexual desire in women.

The hormone some men but mostly women discuss over a hot cup of coffee is estrogen. It is responsible for a woman's development and characteristics. The loss of estrogen can result in lingering symptoms such as hair loss, decreased sexual appetite, or low libido (lacking energy).

Some prefer not to be touched. Without warning, this can happen, even during the time of intimacy. Her body is undergoing changes. While this isn't a pleasant time, she may attempt to fulfill her marriage duties when she really doesn't feel like it. She may find herself going through the motions.

With the loss of estrogen, women have reported that they go through periods of feeling lonely, depressed and having low self-esteem. Men, likewise suffer from low self-esteem when they are not able to perform. Men are challenged in their manhood when they cannot perform at a level that he and his wife are accustomed to. The dissatisfaction can occur for both of the partners, when one is ready and the other is not.

The danger in these things occurring too often is a loss of physical attraction for their mate. Now, it's adjustment time! Remember physical intimacy includes hugging, cuddling, kissing, and holding hands, all while saying sweet words, saying poems to one another.

Some older couples have learned the secret of how to keep the physical intimacy alive as sexual performance is declining. They have learned that there is yet fulfillment as they mature together. They still enjoy one another's company on the oceanfront. They still enjoy holding hands while walking or sitting on the balcony.

Sensitive to the Needs of My Mate

Your desire should always include what can I do to build the esteem of my wife. Hold her hand still. When she is experiencing difficult days, when she is just not up for the physical performance, hold her hand, kiss and hug her. I understand, you are a man and you want to be physical. Your desire is to be with your wife. Some have this response, "what about my needs"? Later with the holding of hands. Brother, sometimes a woman's body goes through these changes for that season of time. Until that time passes, you have to be sensitive.

When Abraham and Sarah begin to go through these changes in their bodies, the Bible talks about not just Abraham not being able to perform, but in Romans fourth chapter it talked about the deadness of Sarah's womb.

What a strong word: deadness. No wonder Sarah responded, "Shall I have pleasure"? During this period of time, Sarah was not performing with Abraham. Sarah gave Abraham her servant. We hear her compromise in Genesis 16:2, "Behold now, the Lord has prevented me from bearing children, go in to my servant; it may be that I shall obtain children by her." According to the custom of that time, when Sarah's servant Hagar became pregnant, the child would belong to Sarah seeing that Hagar was her property.

Needless to say, the times have changed. You won't see wives in 2024 suggesting that their husband go into their servant as Sarah did. Abraham was 86 years old when Hager bore Ishmael. Today, challenges such as prostate problems, high blood pressure, high cholesterol, drugs, Peyronie's disease, depression, smoking and alcohol use contribute to impotency or erectile dysfunction. Husbands have greater physical intimacy as they age when they are healthy.

At 86 years of age, Abraham's body was still making testosterone. He was still able to generate sperm. Hager obviously visited his tent over a period of time. At a time when her body was ovulating, she became pregnant.

Sarah, not able to produce a child, is angered. She was aggravated. Sarah was annoyed the more as Hagar is now strutting and prancing around the house like she has one up on her mistress. Imagine her sashaying around the house saying, "I got your man, I got your man."

And Sarah Prayed

And Sarah prayed or at least she meditated, "one more time, just one more time". "If that hussy gets on my nerves, one more time, I'm going to go upside her head." And finally, she approached Abraham demanding that he get Hagar out of her house. She emphasized how urgent this should be done. "Look homie, you already know, I'm half crazy. Get her out of here, NOW".

Initial Reluctance

At the inception of Sarah's request, there was some reluctance on Abraham's part. Abraham lingered a bit. A soul tie had formed between Abraham and Hager. The time spent together trying to conceive, bonded them. His slow response had something to do with his emotional tie to Hagar.

I pray that those of you desiring to get married will learn something from this untimely inconvenience. Relationships are never easy. Relationship bliss requires some prerequisites. Before you enter into a relationship with a new person, the "tie" (intimate, intense connection) that you had before, needs to be broken. As I mentioned before, I was married. I was connected spiritually before my ex-wife and I were divorced. I had to be healed. For 17 years, I was emotionally connected and mentally connected. I needed to be healed. How bad did I want the healing God had for me?

For me, it was necessary to do the strenuous thing of going on a 21 day fast with water and juice. I'm not instructing you nor suggesting that your situation requires the same. I am, however, asking you "How bad do you want it"? How necessary is it for you to heal before you attempt to enter into another relationship, broken?

The Lord had not finished blessing me, no matter how many times I asked Him, Why me? I needed to prepare to receive His blessing as a blessing. I couldn't connect with the new without disconnecting fully from the old.

Hard Truth

Some of you did not break that soul tie! The person that you were with sexually from the past, you did not break it 100%. And now you are measuring your mate, or comparing what you had before, unable to fully appreciate and receive the new thing.

You must break the soul tie!

For we dare not make ourselves of the number, or compare ourselves with some that commend themselves; but they measuring themselves by themselves, and comparing themselves among themselves are not wise.

I Corinthians 10:12

Always a dilemma. Forever a dispute. Vicious cycles in the relationship because of the unbroken soul tie. Constantly comparing what you had to what you have. While you may be thinking this is not you, these **UNWISE** comparisons can be done consciously or unconsciously.

It is unhealthy for a wife to expect her husband or for a husband to expect his wife to perform like those you were with before. When the old soul tie still exists you will compare what you liked, his or her performance and all things concerning how compatible they were with you. In moments of disagreement, in order to score against their partner, some have gone so far as to say, "You can't do it like…"

Your mate may not be as sexually active as what you're used to. It is unwise for you to compare her performance, expecting to do all the things that were done by other women you have experienced.

Some men are so challenged with physical and emotional intimacy that while engaging in intercourse with their wife, they found themselves thinking that they were with an old partner. Their frustration was that the person that they were with could not do the things that the person before did. The soul-tie has to be broken, even for some of you who have been married for a season.

The ax lies ready at the root of the trees… (St. Matthew 3:10). Therefore, every tree that does not bring forth good fruit is hewn down… There is no hope of bringing forth good fruit, if the axe is not laid at roots remaining from the old relationship. Unless the ax is laid at the root, husbands and wives will continue to be frustrated with the person that you have now.

What Do I Do with My Needs?

For years, women in the body of Christ have honored the Lord by presenting their body as a living sacrifice. These women have submitted themselves to God and have been preserved for 10, 15 and 20 years. As faithful as they were, their life was not without challenges as they waited for a mate. In recent conversations, certain challenges were communicated regarding their needs. The unspoken question in the room was,

"While I wait, is it okay for me to _____. Am I permitted to _____?" These women needed to be reminded that while God understood that they had needs, it did not give them the right to substitute toys in the absence of a man nor fulfill themselves in other ways sexually.

Simultaneously, men waiting on the Lord, do not have permission to watch, read or listen to pornographic material. To entertain pornographic material when married, you begin to commit emotional adultery. Pornographic material sets in motion passion, fleshly affections and sinful lusts. David pursued Bathsheba when he saw her with no clothes on. He wanted what he saw. What he saw looked good. She appealed to him. (II Samuel 11:1-4)

As a Roaring Lion

I encourage you to be watchful! You don't have to inadvertently go looking for the wrong fulfillment. We live in an over-sexualized culture. When unsolicited pictures (nudes) were sent to me. I recognized the devil's tactic and exposed it to my mate. I wanted my wife to be aware of this foolishness. In doing so, I reaffirmed to her that my only want and desire was for her.

You can't expect to take fire in your bosom and not get burned. (Proverbs 6:27-28) It is a dangerous thing to entertain or give place to pornography. The images give rise to seducing thoughts. I know what it is to be single and saved, also. I waited seven years before getting married when I was first born again. I had to quote scriptures like Job 31:1 – I made a covenant with mine eyes: Why then should I think upon a maid? The fight grew intense so I reminded myself of St.

Matthew 5:28 – but I say unto you, that whosoever looketh on a woman to lust after her hath committed adultery with her already in his heart. "I cannot look upon a woman with lust." You have to quote Exodus 20:14 that says, "Thou shall not commit adultery."

I know a beloved couple, the husband being a pastor, almost split when he found out that his wife was committing emotional adultery. Yes, the husband is a pastor. That just goes to show that the enemy will devour anyone whenever an opportunity is given to him. She began to think about this person who she was with, in the past. She began to throw out comments there about this person: what this person could do vs what her husband couldn't do. This almost ripped the marriage to shreds. It was required of this pastor and many other men who have had similar situations to work on their mind, their will and emotions. Imaginations from this type of abuse does not cease on its own. The individual has to cast down imaginations. I can't say for sure how long, at what frequency, nor the number of re-occurrences of these imaginations. I will say that you must be willing to put in the work. Be diligent and plead the blood of Jesus over your mind.

Silence Is Compliance

"Your silence is compliance. It's compliance." Don't give your consent. When someone is looking at you, in a way that they shouldn't, expose it, or call it out to your mate. Make your mate aware of it, even if it is happening at church. Don't call out the person's name because you don't want to create an argument, but you want to expose it. Your silence is compliance. It's easy to yield to the attention and words being said about you at work. Those words can begin to make you feel good, especially when women begin to go through the post-menopausal stages. She wants to feel good, but her metabolism has declined. A woman wants to feel good, but the weight is accumulating. Since the children, she has not had the time to burn it off as intended. She just wants to feel good. Brother, you can't just stop not wanting to be with your wife or move in with another woman just because your wife gained weight. This is an attack on her self-esteem.

Intimacy Intelligence

This section is for grown people. Sarah's decline left her unable to conceive. It was "during the time of life, that she was able to produce." Sarah went from inactive to active. Just as the angels had said. She produced the promised seed of Isaac. During seasons of decline, you have to decide to make adjustments when it comes to physical performance. Ignorance permanently closes doors that could be opened with medication. It's up to the couple to pursue knowledge, drop any embarrassment, sit down together and learn as much as you can.

Learn as much as you can about erectile dysfunction. Learn as much as you can about hypoactive sexual disorder. Men have to learn some of these terms about what a woman's body goes through when she doesn't feel like being touched or when she goes through a season that she just doesn't want to participate in intercourse. Be sensitive when she is emotionally, mentally and physically disconnected. Recognize when she is just going along with you, as not to defraud you, but is really not in the mood.

Learn to value each other more, even when your sexual performance has peaked for the evening. Learn how to talk about how you feel when the desire of one mate is met or reciprocated by the other immediately.

There are times when your body can't perform and you need medical help, assistance, in the form of medicine. Too much of anything is not good for you. Make sure you don't become addicted. I encourage you to go to the doctor. I am not a doctor. The physician or nurse practitioner will be able to assist you in determining if there are underlying causes, so that you can get the medical attention you need.

You make time for what is important to you. Making adjustments include scheduling time to be intimate. Making adjustments, incorporate times of building one of the other three pillars of relationship: EMOTIONAL INTIMACY. Be willing to put in the work. Build in the area of mental and intellectual intimacy. Even when there is a decline in physical intimacy, communicate with your mate, get some knowledge, and agree to see a physician. It will be worth your investment. Remember to incorporate those things that too many consider to be lame. There are rewards to hugging, cuddling, kissing and holding hands.

Men, don't allow the opinions of other men to suggest that these acts are corny, outdated or uncool. You are not hen-pecked because you see the need to enhance the way your woman fills. Holding hands might not meet your needs, but it might keep your wife smiling. Going the extra mile helps to alleviate tension and reminds your queen of her worth.

Father,

*I bless You for this opportunity! You have entrusted
me to bring this word to Your people. I pray that
whatever I have done or ministered to Your people
in word and deed, I did it all unto the glory of God.
Thank you for the results. Thank You for taking our
marriages to the next level of love.*

In Jesus' name, Amen.

Balancing the Different Traditions While Parenting in a Marriage

"For Mature Audiences Only"

Teaching and Preferring YOUR Own Traditions

"Howbeit in vain do they worship me, teaching for doctrines the commandments of men. For laying aside the commandment of God, ye hold the tradition of men as, the washing of pots and cups and many other such things you do."

And he said unto them, "Full well ye reject the commandment of God, that ye may keep our own tradition."

St. Mark 7:7-9

Rebelling and Complaints Against God

It's easy to lose count of the numerous times that the children of Israel rebelled against God. As if one act of rebellion wasn't enough, their complaining reached into the double digits. Moses, who's approach is according to the loving kindness of God, petitioned Him to pardon the people.

And now I beseech thee, let the power of my
Lord be great, according as thou hast spoken,
saying, "The Lord is long-suffering and of great
mercy, forgiven iniquity and transgression, and
by no means clearing the guilty, visiting the
iniquities of the fathers upon the children and to
the third and fourth generation."Pardon, (the
Lord says), I beseech thee, the iniquity of these
people according to the greatness of thy mercy
and has forgiven his people from Egypt until
now. And the Lord said, "I have pardon
according to thy word."

Numbers 14:17-20

Parenting Styles Handed Down Through Traditions

When I call to remembrance the unfeigned faith
that is in thee, which dwelt first in thy
grandmother Lois, and thy mother Eunice; and
I am persuaded that in thee also.

II Timothy 1:5

Paul called to remembrance the authentic, earnest, unforced faith of young Timothy. "It dwelt first in thy grandmother Lois", passing along or handed down from one generation to another. Even so with us, the parenting styles of previous generations affect, form, sway and shape the way many parent their children today. I believe it is safe to say that in some areas, we "do what we've been taught." Without a tutorial or a scheduled sit down by parents or grandparents, they taught us. Examples were left for us. Some of those examples were good while others were not. Some traditions have more influence than others. Sometimes you can see a thing done for so long that it can look like it's right.

Let us define the word tradition.

1. Tradition is the transmission of customs and beliefs from generation to generation.
2. It is a belief or behavior, a custom passed down within a group or a society.
3. A tradition can be a way of thinking, behaving, or doing something in the same pattern as you have been taught, or that which you have seen before you.

We're going to define the word learn.

- Learning is simply gaining or acquiring knowledge or skill by study, by experience, or by being taught. Let me be the first to confess, I have been taught some wrong ways of parenting. As a matter of fact, we all have. We have seen and perpetuated (repeated) pain, simply because certain traditions were not unlearned in time. Some are still affected by the things we learned. The damage was done but it doesn't have to be permanent.

Four Parenting Styles

1. The Authoritative Parenting Style

When the parenting style partly consists of you setting:
- firm rules
- clear guidelines and
- reasonable expectations

An emotional connection is fostered between the parent and the child. These children can go on to develop healthy friendships and relationships on their own due to the safe and trustworthy environment that they were reared in.

This "Authoritative Style" is the gift that keeps on giving!

2. The Rigid Parenting Style

A very different parenting style exist where the authoritarian is generally rigid. Some of us grew up under this rigid parenting style where unreasonable expectations and frequent criticism was the norm.

The safe and trustworthy environment was replaced by an atmosphere where "firm rule" governed the day. Imagine a world where parents set firm rules with little regard, consideration or explanation. The idea of living with a dictator or a strict disciplinarian is very similar. This parenting style could contribute to mental health issues. What's the likelihood of this child becoming a bully?

It is the weed that keeps on growing!

As much as some of us would deny it, the parenting style which we were subjected to affected us and still impacts us even now that we are grown. Remember Beloved, you can see something done wrong for so long, it can look like it's right.

3. The Permissive Parenting Style

The permissive parenting style mirrors a "free-range" style of parenting. It can be both un-restricting and less intense. This is where the parent eases up on the child depending on their individual need. Children have been known to strive in this type of atmosphere. They can become independent.

On the flip side of that, some children need more attention. This parenting style can cause a child to become highly anxious and insecure due to the lack of attachment of a parent. It is the parent responsibility to instill a sense of safety and self-confidence in the child. The child needs to know that he or she can rely on the parents and be assured that they will never be abandoned. No two children are alike. It's okay to operate with a permissive style of parenting when you are able to differentiate when the child may need a little hand holding.

Be willing to make adjustments, giving the proper attention to the individual's (child's unique) bent (interest, desires, passions and giftings). All children are not wired the same. There are different levels of comprehension. One child may grasp understanding or process a matter quicker than another. Even our learning styles can be different. Parents, don't be slack in training them up. God will give you grace and patience.

4. Uninvolved Parenting Style

Imagine growing up in an atmosphere where your parents blessed you financially and purchased clothes at your request. Envision having access to the finer things in life, including the best family vacations. When the parents are uninvolved and do not provide time for the child, however good it appears, it's all an illusion.

And I asked my wife, "Grace", and with careful consideration Grace says, "Love is spelled T-I-M-E"! They want memorable occasions. They're not going to remember that pair of Jordans, you bought them. They're going to remember that time when you brought him on the trip or that time when you showed her how to build a dollhouse. Your son will remember the things you showed him how to put together, stuff around the house. They will remember "those" times.

Time Speaks Volumes

More often than we would like to admit, children are affected by the uninvolved parenting style. In the mind of the child, the parent was unconcerned, disinterested or distant. Even for some of you, your parent(s) were simply not there. Due to the lack of attention given by the parent, a number of children regrettably had to rear themselves. Although you may have dressed better than all the kids in your class, what you really wanted was love; and time equates to love in the lives of people.

Imagine a family living in a nice neighborhood where many of the lawns are manicured and the average income range of the families are from the 120s to 160K. Now imagine a mother who worked 40 hours a week as a nurse while holding down another job on the weekend. The majority of her awake time was away from the home. It appeared to matter that she was able to provide cars for her children at age 16. It seemed to matter that they rarely had to go without tangible things.

All those hours of continual absence played a major role in the rejection and the abandonment experienced by the children over a lengthy period. Instead of having their mother to look to, they related more to an aunt as a mother figure. The son eventually made a decision to enlist in the military as the daughter went off to college. Now they are making a living for themselves. They are no longer relying on their mother's provision.

Who knew that the mother would end up with health challenges? No one could have predicted that the mother would be laying in a hospital bed, challenged with cancer. She wanted to see her son. She desired to see her daughter. They were grown now. There was nothing tangible that tied them to their mother. Oh, the impact and the influence of not being involved when it counts. It's hard to win a city when the walls are fortified with rejection and abandonment.

It is hard to believe that a parent would set out to be uninvolved! Yet it happens every day, even in ministry. As important as it is to hold a position in the church or be highly respected in your community, making provision for your family should not be disregarded. Beloved, it is my belief that when we get to heaven, we will be judged a lot more for what we did, or didn't do in our family's life.

> *But if any provide not for his own, and specially*
> *for those of his own house, he hath denied the*
> *faith, and is worse than an infidel.*
>
> *I Timothy 5:8*

As we busy ourselves, pursuing our call to ministry and placing a significant amount of time branding (a name for the selling of goods and services) and working our jobs, let us stop and consider the value of investing in family. Political affiliations and other endeavors that produce the accolades of men, shouldn't be primary.

Calling all Christians...

Don't allow yourselves to be outdone by unbelievers, who designate time with their families. I think it's time that we give ourselves to nourishing our children beyond that once a year, seven-day vacation that was set up for your enjoyment more so than theirs.

Now That They Are Grown

Being grown does not undo what was done. Some of our grown children were affected by what occurred. The things that transpired in their youth is producing an unpleasant harvest.

Divorce and separation can produce various degrees of challenges. Unfaithfulness in a marriage, by either the husband or the wife will open doors. If the husband or wife rejects or abandons the children, it can have an effect on them when they are grown.

Parenting styles have lingering, long-lasting effects. You could be 60 or 70 years of age. You could be 30 to 40 years of age and still be affected by the constant day to day activity that controlled the household you grew up in. Aging has not been a deterrent. In spite of all the years that have passed, the damage experienced by the things you heard and saw still negatively affects many. Traditions have been established. From one generation to another, ways of behaving have become the norm. Many families develop a culture of believing without ever challenging a stronghold that existed on the blood line for many generations.

Beloved, we have to always remember seedtime and harvest time exist regardless of what is sown. If the "errors" was sown in one generation, the adversary is counting on a harvest in the next.

While the earth remaineth, seedtime and harvest, and cold and heat, and summer and winter, and day and night shall not cease.

Genesis 8:22

Many years ago, I was instructed by God to take authority over the spirit of adultery. God commanded me to go on a fast and take authority over this spirit. My reply to God was, I'm not thinking about committing adultery. I'm happy that you blessed me with a wife. I'm just so grateful.

Beloved, as believers…

> *Christ has redeemed us from the curse of the law, being made a curse for us: for it is written, Cursed is everyone that hangeth on a tree: that the blessing of Abraham might come on the Gentiles through Jesus Christ; that we might receive the promise of the Spirit through faith.*
>
> *Galatians 3:13-14*

Christ has unapologetically redeemed us from every curse. As a result of disobedience, doors are open for things that operated on the bloodline (patterns that operated in generations before). It is our responsibility to shut the door.

Papa was a rolling stone.
Wherever he laid his hat was his home.
And when he died
All he left us was (Alone)...
The Temptations

How true were the words of this song regarding the father of someone I know. Like the lyrics of this song, the spirit of adultery on his father's life desired to replicate itself in his life. It operated in generations before, even in his grandfather and desired to have him. What operated on the blood-line wanted to stay in the region. It was up to him to shut the doors by declaring war. Because he didn't want to be subjected to the same spirit of adultery, he went on a seven-day fast and broke the power of this spirit from operating in his life.

That was his father and that was his grandfather who he loved. He loved them and yet he suffered from the pain he experienced from their behavior pattern. The repercussion of generational decisions really does create consequences when left unchecked.

Jesus redeemed him. What operated freely in previous generations could not legally overpower him to act according to the patterns of the past. But with a vengeance, that same spirit of adultery wanted to produce wounds and affect his children. Like a ripple effect, when doors are unchecked in one mate or the other, some level of access is granted to the children. So is the case with some of you and/or some of your children who are grown.

God help the child. Lord, help the children who are suffering from the things (deeds, actions, observations) and words they heard us utter) before we were born again. You may be asking yourself what does those things of the past have to do with me, today? What good will come out of me revisiting it? Could it be possible that the Lord would perform a work of deliverance in your grown children by using you to sincerely apologize to them? Beloved, true remorse manifests when correction is given. It's time for many ungodly doors to be shut by parents who are now born again and filled with the Holy Spirit and whose desire is to see their grown children set free also.

Romans, chapter 8 says it clearly, "There is no condemnation to those who are in Christ Jesus…" If you have given your life to Christ and asked your children for forgiveness, there is no criticism. If you've apologized to them and asked the Lord to create in you a clean heart for the things done, then God has truly forgiven you. However, the children may still be affected by the sinful behavior that was modeled before them and by a cantankerous atmosphere.

Seed-Time

Like reverberations, there are direct and indirect consequences. It happened in a period described as **SEED-TIME**! Like reverberations, the impact of the seeds sown can last for a long time. I believe Genesis 8:22 is worth mentioning again: "While the earth remaineth, seedtime and harvest, and cold and heat, and summer and winter, and day and night shall not cease."

In looking at the family line of Abraham, Isaac, Jacob, all the way down to Joseph, we will see behaviors of one generation "opening doors", introducing destructive attitudes, giving access to spiritual enemies which had early plans of suffering for the next generation. Sometimes it's hard to admit that even righteous people can make wrong choices because of what is taught to them.

Thoughts of peace and not of evil, to give you an expected end. (Jeremiah 29.11). God desires to bless generations through obedience. God blessed Timothy and showed up in his life. That unfeigned faith in his life dwelt first in preceding generations. It was recognizable in his grandmother Lois and patterned before his mother Eunice. It was their persuasion and influence that became the cornerstone for Timothy's faith that would neither decline, regress (retreat), nor digress.

Thank God for the tutelage of Lois and Eunice. Bravo to prior generations that were strong enough to endure when contradictions and hardships showed up to discourage or cause the next generation to deviate from the path of God. Be not weary in well doing. Continue to take them to Sunday school. Vacation Bible School does make a difference. Christian summer camp and attendance to Christian schools does help.

The same God that blessed Timothy through generations, is blessing young children and children who are now grown. Lois endured and Eunice endured. They were able to pass down generational blessings by illustrating and being an example by which Timothy could pattern himself during times of uncertainty. Not only was Timothy "told", but he was taught. He was able to observe their experience at home.

Children are a heritage of the Lord: and the fruit of the womb is his reward. As arrows are in the hand of a mighty man; so are children of the youth. Happy is the man that hath his quiver full of them; they shall not be ashamed, but they shall speak with the enemies in the gate. (Psalm 127:3-5). This is a God ideal. Children are not ascribed in many cultures as a reward. They are not considered as a heritage of the Lord, but rather a burdened or another mouth to feed.

It takes a mighty man, as opposed to a man immersed in other priorities, to aim the children in the direction of God. The unselfish acts of the mighty man shut the door (access, entrance, intrusion, invasions) on all generational transmitted behaviors and practices attempting to perpetuate themselves.

I'm so glad that God is able to redeem! He is the same yesterday, today and forever. (Hebrews 13:8). There is no restraint on God and His ability to reach back and heal pains of the past. God knows what happened and how it affected the family.

But Righteous People Can Make Wrong Choices

Before we begin to boast about the steps of a righteous man, let us first consider what was taught to us. Can it be true? Can righteous people make wrong choices? The course of action that you took was based on the tutors in your life. If the tutors were not competent then the actions that you took were limited by your understanding.

Beloved, many of us didn't do, because we didn't know. And when we thought to consider what was written, we found another law in our members, warring against the law of our mind (Romans 7:23). What was taught by these tutors left of wanting...

You were taught!
> Taught through abuse
> Taught through abandonment
> Taught through rejection
> Taught through acts of favoritism shown to another sibling
> Yes, you were taught!
> And yes, you need to be healed.

Favoritism in the House

Isaac and Rebecca had the two sons Jacob and Esau. The Bible says that Jacob was Rebecca's son, and it says that Esau was Isaac's son.

The parents began to show favoritism over their children. One parent has a preference for one child over the other. And with that preference came preferential treatment, bias and maybe a hint of unfairness. This is exactly how it is viewed in the eyes of the child who may be starving for attention.

Let's take a look at the decision made by Rebecca in Genesis 27:1-4. She made a decision when Isaac was beginning to die that affected the household.

And it came to pass, that when Isaac was old, and his eyes were dim so that he could not see, he called Esau his eldest son, and said unto him, "My son; and he said unto him, Behold here am I. And he said, Behold now, I am old, I know not the day of my death: Now therefore take, I pray thee, they weapons, thy quiver and thy bow, and go out to the field, and take me some venison; And make me savoury meat, such as I love, and bring it to me, that I may eat; that my soul may bless thee before I die.

Genesis 27:1-4

Bad choices were made. Rebecca began to assist Jacob in obtaining the blessing. Jacob had already been a trickster because he tricked his brother Esau for a morsel of bread; he sold his birthright. The word of God says, but then his mother, Rebecca, who favored Jacob over Esau..."

Today, the favoring of one child over the next can be defined as disapproval for the other. All the acts of kindness for one child can be perceived as neglect by children who feels overlooked. That lack of affirmation can show up as low self-esteem in the other child.

A parent can express favor for one child over another because one attended college and obtained a degree verses the other who didn't. A child can be left unnoticed while another child gets all the attention because they are more attractive. The results are the same. This seed of favoritism most often damages the child and manifest, itself in the form of rejection.

Jacob's mother; Jacob's own mother assisted him in stealing the blessing away from Esau. Why didn't Jacob object? Why didn't he speak up? Why was he so willing, to go along with the plan? It obviously felt good to be in his mom's good graces. Sometimes a child can come in agreement with a parent if favoritism is shown. Instead of drawing attention to the unfair behavior and pointing out the obvious effects of the ill or mistreatment of their sibling, in that moment they are motivated by their own need for validation.

Without a doubt, Esau was affected as his own mother conspired with Jacob in tricking Issac to release the blessing that would otherwise be his. How damaged was Esau? His own mother, who already loved his brother more than him, once again was used to inflict major pain in his life. "And when Esau heard the words of his father, he cried with a great and exceeding bitter cry... "(Genesis 27:34)

"For ye know how that afterward, when he would have inherited the blessing, he was rejected: for he found no place of repentance, though he sought it carefully with tears (Hebrews 12:17). Rebecca's heavy influence is often overshadowed by Jacob's name which means trickster. How many times have we skimmed over Genesis 27:8 - Now therefore, my son, obey my voice according to that which I command thee. And Rebecca began to give instructions to be carried out by Jacob. We can easily see now, how his identify was defined by the behavior patterns, the mindsets and the deceptive actions of the generation before him. Evidence of this influence is further revealed in the deceptive means of Leban, Jacob's uncle on his mother's side.

Jacob was on the run from an angry Esau, who vowed to kill him. He arrived at his uncle Laban's place where he served for seven years for the Rachel, the woman that he originally fell in love with. Jacob wanted her from the time he saw her at a well. When the seven years were fulfilled, and the time had come to consummate the marriage in the tent, Jacob was surprised as instead of Rachel, Laban had switched his older daughter Leah, who was not as fair as Rachel. Jacob ended up with the sister who was teary-eyed or cross-eyed. The wrong woman was in the tent.

Like brother, like sister. How familiar is the behavior of Leban to that of his sister Rebecca. This evil from one generation is showing up in the next. Unless these doors of influence are closed, generations will become vulnerable to experience the same. Even Joseph, Rebecca's son was a victim of the same.

When Will the Bleeding Stop?

Jacob committed to serving seven more years for Rachel's hand in marriage. After 14 years, Jacob had two wives, yet he favored Rachel over Leah.

… And the two wives of Jacob began to have children. Rachel was left not bearing for a while. Leah on the other hand, began to bear. In the fulness of time God opened Rachel's womb and she gave birth to Joseph and later Benjamin. Altogether, the two sisters and their servants Bilhah's and

Zilpah bore Joseph 12 sons and one daughter. Jacob favored Joseph over his other sons. Genesis 37:4, declares, "When Joseph's brothers saw that their father loved him more than any of them, they hated him…" Here we see another generation affected.

Here is another generation, where the pain of rejection, lack of acknowledgement and hunger for affirmation would have free course, if not dealt with appropriately. Oh, how it affected the other 10 sons, in various degrees. No one would have ever considered that it could promote hatred among the brothers.

Rachel in the process of giving birth to Benjamin, died. As the brothers grew, it was obvious that their father's affection was toward their brother Joseph. **THEY SAW IT**. It would have been enough that Jacob gave Joseph a coat of many colors, but to top it off, Joseph began to tell them of his dreams that fanned the flames for envy and anger.

The hurt they held on to, similar to the hurt some of us held on to, moved them to conspire against their brother. In the same manner, some of our children may carry resentment toward a sibling. When they would be allies, the hurt causes them to be enemies.

Conspiracy in the House

Come now therefore, and let us slay him and cast him into some pit (Genesis 37:20). They ripped up his coat of many colors, and they put blood on him to make it appear that some evil beast hath devoured him. They threw him down into a pit. It was Reuben that delivered him out of their hands, saying,

"Let us not kill him". Judah spoke up among the brothers, seeing little profit slaying him and concealing his blood.

It just so happened to be Midianites merchantmen passing by, who drew and lifted up Joseph from the pit and sold Joseph to the Ishmaelites, for twenty pieces of silver. Reuben returned to the pit and saw that Joseph was missing. Some theologians believed that God, because of His sovereign plan, had those Ishmaelites to come by to get Joseph to the place that his gift would make room for him.

Jacob cries, renting of his clothes, putting on of sackcloth nor mourning for Joseph, could undo the wrong that was done by his brothers. Parents can create mess, confusion and disharmony among their children. Whenever this occurs in a family it sets children against their own siblings. Favoritism can foster ill feeling among siblings that prevent them from speaking to one another. There are underlying reasons why one won't come to the cookout, or other family gatherings. Internalized pain can be the cause.

Even after you said, "Please forgive me," it wasn't enough. Sometimes healing has to take its course. Your admittance however, can be the very thing needed to create the shift in the process.

The Situation Will Not Correct Itself

A word of wisdom: You can't go to the person who hurt you or afflicted you for advice or to help you change. Jacob's sons could not go to him for help. Jacob was the one who inflicted the pain in the first place. Unless he owned what he contributed to the situation, there would be no healing for his sons. If there was any hope of correcting, it would require

Jacob. Jacob never corrected it. Such is the case in many family scenarios, the parent fails to correct it.

Simeon and Levi are brethren; instruments of cruelty… (Genesis 49:5). Jacob called his sons together to tell them what shall befall them. Instead of blessing them, Jacob cursed their anger. Dina their sister had been violated (raped). Jacob did not do anything at that time. Two years had passed before Simeon and Levi, boiling with rage, took matters into their own hands. Daddy isn't doing anything! Why won't he give his attention to this dishonoring of our sister? Children begin to wonder why something is done for one child and nothing is done for next. Why would a parent jump through hoops to correct a matter concerning one child and show little activity when it comes to the next. Is it not a show of favoritism and neglect?

When Is Daddy Going to Do Something?

Shechem, the man that raped Dina, and his father wanted their families to come together. Two years passed and Jacob hadn't done anything to correct the situation. He didn't do anything! What Jacob said to Shechem's father, if your men will be circumcised, then we will allow them to come into our daughters and our sons can go into their wives.

In the meantime, anger and bitterness had crept in. Jacob's delay in correcting the problem gave Simeon and Levi too much time to consider a plan of action of avenging themselves. But when the grown men were circumcised, Levi and Simeon expressed their outrage, took their swords, went throughout the camp and they killed all the men because their sister was raped. In their minds, somebody had to avenge their sister since daddy didn't.

Were their actions, right? No. Did Jacob teach them to handle matters this way? No. In the midst of his delayed response, doors of anger and jealousy opened. A door for destructiveness opened and Jacob did not correct it. Because he did not shut the door, everyone was affected.

In Conclusion...

- For all of you who have had a parent speak negatively over you...
- For any of you who have developed a habit of speaking about yourself in a negative way...
- For you who have had curses spoken over you...
- For those reading who have been damaged emotionally...

You can forgive today. Forgiveness is your decision. Deciding to forgive releases you from the bondage that tries to tie you to revenge, bitterness, hatred, and malice. You no longer have to live subject to those harsh words. You can renounce those hidden things of dishonesty and pain that attempted to flow through your family lineage.

Don't leave the door cracked! Close the door completely. Don't be afraid to acknowledge the obvious pattern in the bloodline. Open your eyes and be willing to deal with what you are seeing repeat itself. Don't allow those destructive patterns to continue. As a new creation in Christ Jesus, you have been redeemed. You are free to enjoy the new realities available to you through your relationship with Him. Having knowledge of things, behaviors, habits, practices, character traits and strongholds of proceeding generations, doesn't make you a victim. The Holy Spirit will keep you alert and cause you to be both watchful and prayerful against any attacks designed to snare the blood-line again.

As much as possible, with the help of the Holy Spirit, reach back and help your children and grandchildren. God wants them healed! Remember again, Romans 8:1. There is no guilt on your part, after you have repented before the Lord. Your child may not respond favorably to your help today. Your apology may not have an immediate impact. Sometimes healing takes place in part. May the Lord give the increase and heal the land.

Grace ... to Be a Eunuch

The disciples said to Him, "If the case of a man with his wife is like this, it is neither profitable nor advisable to marry."

Jesus was clear when He replied, **"NOT ALL MEN CAN ACCEPT THIS SAYING."** (In other words, this teaching does not apply to everyone, but only to those who God has given it.) *For there are different reasons why men cannot marry: some, because they were born that way; others, because men made them that way; and others do not marry for the sake for the Kingdom of heaven. Let him who can accept this teaching do so."*

St. Matthew 19:10-12

This scripture is often glossed over because from a young age, the idea of marriage is introduced. Princes and Princesses were excited about marriage and happily-ever-afters long before social media were introduced to young kids. To deny oneself the opportunity of getting married for the sake of the Kingdom of Heaven is archaic. Besides, who can accept this?

The term Eunuch is old-school. It is an old English word that is not mentioned very much in our time. Jesus however used the term. We will use the word eunuch interchangeably with celibacy and abstinence, even though they can sometimes vary.

Eunuch – A man who has been castrated and is incapable of reproducing. His occupation was usually one in charge of a harem, a place where women were protected, kept, or employed. A Eunuch would give himself fully to the act of servitude. Because he was not married, he could give himself to the things that belonged to the Lord and how he may please God (I Corinthians 7:32-35). Paul helps us to understand this choice, inhibiting certain distractions that would otherwise occur for those choosing to be a husband or father. He could give undivided devotion to the Lord.

Celibacy – The state of abstaining (refrain, renounce, decline) from marriage and sexual relations.

Abstinence – Restraining oneself from indulgence. This type of restraint is self-enforced.

For the servant who chose the lifestyle of a eunuch during the days of Christ is no different than those who would serve God in that compacity today. It is still for the kingdom of God. The word may not be a part of our vernacular but the idea of serving God in that capacity is no stranger to those who are graced to present their bodies in honor to God.

Cultural Differences

In different cultures around the world some are deemed "female natural eunuchs." These women give their ovaries or have their uterus removed or both, so that they cannot bear children. They too desire to fulfill their duties without the distraction of a husband or children. This practice is prevalent today in the country of India, where there are about one million eunuchs. Can you imagine such a large population of people who have undergone certain natural things, just so that they can serve under political authority or for religious reasons? In North America, there are as many as 600,000 men living as eunuchs for medical reasons. Many of them have been affected by prostate cancer. I was surprised to learn that medical procedures were undergone by men to decrease testosterone to prevent the metastasizing (spreading) of this disease.

Natural Eunuchs, What About Them?

Most of you have never considered giving yourself as a natural eunuch. Celibacy is a difficult subject for the stomach. The big "A" word, ABSTINENCE, has been unchartered territory for great lengths of time. Many excuses have been made for dishonoring the lord, only for an occasion to indulge again. "For the sake of the Kingdom," is sometimes just church jargon (lingo) and nothing more.

Exactly what was Jesus talking about when he referred to those who made themselves eunuchs for the sake of the kingdom? After careful study and deliberation, I found that Christ was speaking of a spiritual commitment made by both men and women and not some procedure such as physical castration, removal of the ovaries and in some cases the uterus. He was referring to that which is of the spirit and not of the flesh. For better understanding, let us look at the following passage:

> *For he is not a Jew, which is one outwardly;*
> *neither is that circumcision, which is outward in*
> *the flesh: but he is a Jew, which is one inwardly;*
> *and circumcision is that of the heart, in the*
> *spirit, and not in the letter; whose praise is not*
> *of men, but of God.*
>
> *Romans 2:28-29*

Many of us will admit that our first notion is to identify the word eunuch with that which is outwardly. Christ is speaking about spiritual circumcision. He is not speaking of the practice of removing the foreskin of males as babies.

Summary:
- For he is not a Jew, which is one outwardly.
- Neither is that circumcision, which is outward of the flesh.
- But he is a Jew, which is one inwardly.
- Circumcision is that of the heart, in the spirit.

He's talking about a circumcision of the spirit and of the heart.

A new heart also will I give you, and a new spirit will I put within you: and I will take away the stony heart out of your flesh, and I will give you a heart of flesh. And I will put my spirit within you, and cause you to walk in my statutes, and ye shall keep my judgments, and do them (Ezekiel 36:26-27).

Not only is Ezekiel referring to having a born-again experience but he is also alluding to the infilling of the Spirit. John increases our understanding by adding in chapter 14 vs 17, "for he dwelleth with you, and shall be in you."

We should stop and take time to specifically give God praise for the work that is being done by the indwelling Spirit of God. There is a stubbornness that resides in our flesh, always in resistance to the circumcision of the heart. This stubbornness, unbelievably, always resists the work of the Lord, you love.

Ezekiel is speaking prophetically, "And you shall keep my judgment,"! There it is, another place where we ought to stop and give God more praise. "And you shall do them!" Praise God! We need all the help that we can get.

Spiritual Circumcision

Paul addresses the church of Philippi... *"FOR WE ARE THE CIRCUMCISION"* (Philippians 3:3). He is addressing both male and female born-again believers. Brethren, a spiritual eunuch can be either male or female. There is nothing so clear as Paul's description of the behavior who had just been identified. He or she is a worshipper.

- Which worship God in the spirit
- And rejoice in Christ Jesus
- And put no confidence in the flesh.

Now that is something to dance about. I would take it by force if I were you. These are words from God about you that you can declare over yourself daily. Beloved, when you choose to embrace a life of celibacy, a life of abstinence, you are putting no confidence in your flesh to keep you. You are putting confidence in the ability of the Almighty God Himself to keep you. Oh God, I bless you. There you go… another opportunity to give God your highest praise. Dear Brother or sister, this book means nothing if you can stop eating for a moment to give God your best, Thank YOU! I am only referring to your victorious life and walk in Christ. When you know the WHO "in" you that makes the difference, then you can be different.

Vows Made for Different Reasons

I'll never get married again! Some have carelessly (rashly, hastily, without careful consideration) expressed it verbally while others have communicated, pledged, or sworn to it non-verbally. Their indifference to marriage stemmed out of a broken relationship where they still bore fragments of anger, frustration, and regret. The individual making this statement set in motion or created an atmosphere where marriage would not be likely.

If an individual embraces a life of celibacy, typically for religious reasons, they are committing to abstaining from marriage or sexual relations. This commitment can be for an extended period or forever.

While both celibacy and abstinence have similarities, it is important to note that celibacy involves making a vow.

> *Better is it that thou shouldest now vow, than*
> *that thou shouldest vow and not pay.*
>
> *Ecclesiastes 5:5*

Celibacy is a vow to the Lord. This can be for an extended period or for the remainder of one's life. Abstinence on the other hand refers to a decision not to have penetrated sex for a period, believing that God will bless you with a future husband or wife. The person willingly constrained or refrained for a period, re-engages when God blesses them after matrimony. Dating does not authorize you to re-engage in physical activities. Until marriage, abstinence is to continue to be exercised.

When You're Doing Too Much!

Keep your focus! Exercise restraint! Close, intimate hugging only feeds the flesh. It is not wise to stir up your flesh before it's time. This includes passionate kissing.

Just because you are grown does not mean you can manage grown up situations. Great kings have fallen, thinking they were grown enough. Many godly women have fallen into seduction, just because they felt they were "grown enough". Remember what we shouted about earlier, "no confidence in the flesh".

This time of engagement is an exciting time to get to know the person that is to be your spouse. You get to see how they interact with you and how you interact with them. That's a lot to take in. It is during this period that you drop unrealistic expectations that derived from a previous relationship. This is your future. Together, you can take advantage of the new things that God will do in one another. Enjoy your time of courting and dating. There are many memories to be made. Don't jump the gun. Don't rush into activities involving sex. Allow your future mate the space for unhealthy soul ties from an old relationship to be broken.

Remember, time before the Lord is necessary! That dedicated time in His presence will allow some purging and renouncing of things you participated in and subjected yourself to. There may be some things you accepted in a previous relationship or deeds practiced that you need to turn away from. By renouncing those actions, you are denouncing any legal claim for those thoughts or desires to interfere with your life going forward. Don't be ashamed. The past doesn't have to own you. Many have fallen into error by comparing their future mate to an old flame from the past. II Corinthians 10 vs 12 says, "…this is unwise." What God joins together foolish comparison won't tear apart.

I speak this to those of you who can receive it. **THE FLESH HAS AN APPETITE**. Don't feed it! It is not wise to allow kissing, fondling, heavy petting or touching of your genital areas. Foreplay will only lead to arousal. I Corinthians 10:12 says, Wherefore let him that thinketh he standeth take heed lest he fall.

Crush those lies that give you permission to awaken love before it's time (Song of Solomon 8:4).

During the Engagement: The Flood

For many, it happened during the engagement. People you know, preachers you know, and some theologians took the bait and fell. Satan has used the same tactics and has not had to reinvent his methods. Some fell, ignorant of the devices while others fell thinking they could outsmart the tactics Satan uses. The enemy timed their compromise and then planted a seed in their mind that it was only a mistake. Truth is, you ignored the red flags.

There is nothing wrong during this engagement period for another set of eyes. For your good, for the good of the person you intend to marry and for the future of your relationship, bring them before authority. Authority should be able to check his or her spirit as well as yours. The authority could be a guardian, your parents, a bishop or an elder, a prophet, an evangelist or one of the spiritual mothers in the church. Their ability to discern can offer much wisdom and caution. The authority figure can bring things to your attention that you could have overlooked. The benefit is often aborted due to attachments made during premarital sex. Instead of seeking out the advice of the elders the young couple rushes to the altar unprepared.

It matters how a couple connects! The Lord taught me years ago the value of prioritizing your spiritual connection. The couple should follow up with connecting soullessly and then physically. Connecting physically first can be self-sabotaging. It can undermine your entire relationship. Don't abort your spiritual connection. Allow this spiritual connection to take place. It will determine if your relationship has the proper foundation.

Frequently Asked Questions

- Am I ever supposed to get married?
- Did I make a mistake by getting married in the first place?
- My mate has gone home to be with the Lord, am I supposed to ever get married again?
- Lord, it has taken so long for me to get married. Am I supposed to?
- Is there something wrong with me that nobody has chosen me by now?

Being uncertain or having a question like those above doesn't make you guilty of sin. These questions and more are on the heart of God's people. The strength of the temptation sometimes can rest in trying to live out the will of God for your life while not knowing "specifically" what it is and too afraid to ask. Come close... God knows the plans He has for you!

"...I am Alpha and Omega, the first and the last"

Revelations 1:11

God knows the beginning of a thing and the end of a things. God knows everything regarding our lives from the beginning to the end.

> *"...There has no temptation that have taken you such as is common to man"*
>
> *I Corinthians 10:13*

It is not unusual for professing believers to endure temptations that are common to man. Endurance, however, does not happen often. Despite the number who yield to temptation, there are others who embrace the mantle of abstinence or clothe themselves with the cloak of celibacy. He will not put or allow more than what you're able to bear. Only those who trust Him see the way or possibilities of escaping.

That You May be Able to Bear It

What a good place to thank God for His consideration for the things we are to bear. Even when we think that we are ready for certain things, God knows what we are capable of handling. We beseech Him with questions that we've already formulated the response. And when we don't get an immediate response, we don't see it as the grace of God.

Beloved, we don't always want to hear what the "good" Lord has to say. I emphasize good because even if He says something different from what you desire to hear, it's always for your best. The best of us is not in favor of hearing God say, "your marriage will end in a divorce, and you will never marry again." That's a hard word when you have given yourself faithfully to a marriage where your spouse was unfaithful. It's not the easiest when due to unreconcilable differences your marriage dissolves and the word of the prophet or pastor is,

171

"Thus says the Lord, you will never marry again." You hang your head in disbelief. Why would God…? I was the faithful one.

So conscious of you and I, is our God. He is your ally, so acquainted with and watchful over your future and heart. He knows how you are impacted by what He says. There are unique times when your prayers reach God without an immediate response. These are the times when God seems silent. He knows that the answer to your question would be too hard for you.

Hannah would testify, it really was a hard thing (I Samuel 1:2-8)! You read (gloss over) it in the scripture, but she had to endure the reality of being barren. May the Lord be with you in a season where you are challenged with hard things. Hard things like, "Thus says the Lord, you will never marry, you will never have children".

Not everyone is waiting on the edge of the pew to hear, "thus says the Lord", from the womb, I have chosen you to live a life committed to me; to remain unmarried and to dedicate your spirit, soul, and body to me for the rest of your life". Not everyone is eager to hear a word like that. God won't give you a word such as that because you're not able to bear it. He will send a word, however, that is mixed with the right amount of grace that helps you to say yes.

Pushy Prayer Request

Was that your prayer request I heard? Are you pushing your way through the line, trying to get God to move on your behalf before He responds to anything else? Beloved, you don't have to be rude for God to attend to your need. Telling the Lord: how long it's taking for you to get married, probably won't speed things up. On and on and on... Lord, I have not had any children. What about my legacy? Is there something wrong with me?

These thoughts are more common than you think, but they don't have to govern your thought life. You should rather give God the praise for preserving you for His purpose. Just because certain desires haven't manifested for you doesn't indicate that "anything is wrong with you". Sometimes the delay is God's way of preserving you for this season.

Three Types of Eunuchs

1. Eunuchs that are made by men.
2. Eunuchs who have made themselves eunuchs for the kingdom.
3. Those that are made eunuchs or who are celibate or abstinent from birth.

Let not the foreigner who has joined himself to
the Lord say, The Lord will surely separate me
from His people. And let not the eunuch say,
Behold, I am a dry tree.

For thus says the Lord: To the eunuchs who
keep My Sabbaths and choose the things which
please Me and hold firmly My covenant – To
them I will give in My house and within My
walls a memorial and a name better [and more
enduring] than sons and daughters; I will give
them an everlasting name that will not be cut
off. Also the foreigners who join themselves to
the Lord to minister to Him and to be His
servants, everyone who keeps the Sabbath so as
not to profane it and who holds fast My
covenant [by conscientious obedience]. All
these I bring to My holy mountain and made
them joyful in My house of prayer. Their burnt
offerings and their sacrifices will be accepted
on My altar; for My house will be called a
house of prayer for all peoples.

Isaiah 56:3-7

- Let not the eunuch or those who chose a life of abstinence, of celibacy, say, behold, I am a dry land.
- Be conscious of how you speak about yourself.
- Don't confess that this is hard.
- Say instead, I can do all things through Christ Who strengthens me.

- Order your conversation aright! Stop speaking of your difference as one who is cursed.
- See yourself through the eyes of God. You are not pitiful!
- If God has chosen this path for you or if you have chosen this mantle for your life then you are not deserving of pity.
- Keep my sabbath, hold firm, and choose those things that please me.

Lord We Want to Please You

"...To them, will I give My house and within My walls a memorial." "...And more enduring than the sons or daughters." "I will give them an everlasting name that would not be cut off." To God be the glory. It fascinates me to see how mindful and regardful God is. Praise God for those that sacrifice and keep His covenant. Praise God for those who through conscientious obedience, hold fast.

God revealed the future by showing the Apostle John 144,000. John's reply was "Who are these'? There was a light on them. They were 144,000 Jews from the 12 tribes of Israel, and they were undefiled Jews. They were men that were chosen, that were eunuchs, that were celibate, who were abstinent for the sake of the kingdom of God. With them there was such a glow, unique and different from all the others seen in heaven.

God recognizes all that we do in honor of Him. He gave recognition to the foreigner who laid down his life. He recognizes and highlight to the Apostle John the 144,000 Jews who served in a special capacity.

God's grace enables you to yield to Him. There is the reward of joy to those who have given themselves to God and taken on the mantle of a Eunuch. For all those who have chosen a life to where you can attend to the Lord without distraction will have joy!!!

Biblical Proof of Eunuchs

Then Isaiah said to Hezekiah, "Hear the word of the Lord! Behold, the time is coming when all that is in your house, and that which your forefathers have stored up till this day, shall be carried to Babylon; nothing shall be left, says the Lord. And some of your sons who shall be born to you shall be taken away, and they shall be eunuchs in the place of Babylon's king.

II Kings 20:16-18

It is believed by some that Shadrack, Meshach, and Abednego, even Daniel, were eunuchs. There is no biblical proof that substantiate it. Acts 8:27 on the other hand confirms the presence of an Ethiopian eunuch (a man who has been castrated), that served under Queen Candace. The scripture declares that he was a court official who oversaw all her treasure. This man, due to the pigment of his skin, is considered by most to be black.

On returning home from Israel for worship, this eunuch had a life changing experience. God used Philip to minister to him the good news about Jesus. ... And as soon as they came to water, the eunuch was baptized. Careful research links the conversion and baptism of the Ethiopian eunuch to the wide spreading of the gospel in Africa.

A Eunuch from Birth

Before I formed in the belly, I knew thee before thou came forth out of the belly, I sanctified thee, and I ordained you a prophet unto the nation.

Jeremiah 1:5

And the word of the Lord came also into me saying, thou shall not take unto thee a wife.

Jeremiah 16:1

Jeremiah was made a "spiritual eunuch", for the purpose of giving his life to the ministry which he was sanctified (set apart). God instructed him to not take a wife nor have sons and daughters. This meant that he had to give himself up to a life of celibacy and abstinence.

God instructed Jeremiah to not take a wife. These words came in a season where he was either at the age where young men customarily choose a wife or close to it. God did not need to speak this word to Jeremiah when he was a little boy. These words were spoken to Jeremiah the man. Jeremiah the man, who was under the tutelage of spiritual teachers, could process or handle the weight of such a word.

Thank God for the spiritual influence and the understanding he had of the scripture. Otherwise like many of us, he would have been crushed by *"THUS SAITH THE LORD."*

There would not have been a need for God to instruct Jeremiah that neither would he have any sons or daughters, in this place, except he had all the tools to produce. He had the ability, but it was not in God's will. In other words, Jeremiah was not castrated. Jeremiah clothed himself with the mantle or cloak of abstinence and/or celibacy.

Mary, Mary, Not Contrary

Consider the life, testimony, and turnaround of one of our favorite characters in the New Testament. Some can't help but focus on Luke's depiction of her in chapter 8 vs 2: and certain women, which had been healed of evil spirits and infirmities, Mary called Magdalene, out of whom went seven devils. If you could ask her what a do-over looked like, she could tell you. If you had the chance to meet her, expecting her to be ashamed, you would be surprisingly disappointed. She had not always lived her best life. Her life, in fact, was promiscuous.

Could the cloak of celibacy and abstinence fit her? The answer depends on who you ask. What can God do with a wild, licentious, unchaste, unrestrained, sexually indiscriminate woman name Mary? She decided, with the help of the Lord, to give herself to the Lord and take on the mantle of a eunuch along with Susanna who ministered their substance to Jesus, along with Joanna who was married. This was all for the sake of the Kingdom.

These women and more, helped finance the Kingdom. They could do it because they embraced a level of life for celibacy. To embrace it, they had to keep themselves busy. Until I come... Apostle Paul says, "give attendance to reading, exhortation, to doctrine (I Timothy 4:13). Remember Jesus' own words, "Mine is to do the will of Him that sent me (John 6:38)."

Anna Takes the Stand

Embracing God's call to embrace this calling takes on a different look when it is an extended period. If anyone can testify of the grace of the mantle of celibacy and abstinence, it would be Anna.

And she coming in that instant gave thanks likewise unto the Lord, and spake of him to all them that looked for redemption in Jerusalem. And when they had performed all things according to the law of the Lord, they returned into Galilee, to their own city Nazareth.

Luke 2:38-39

Anna was a woman of great age. She had a husband, seven years of her virginity (Luke 2:36). She had been married seven years and then she was a widow. Women were considered mature enough to marry at earlier ages. According to the culture of that time, she was believed to be around the age of 13 or 14, like the age of Jesus' mother before she had a child.

And Anna was young too. After seven years her husband died. If Anna's age ranged between 14 and 18, after seven years, she would have been between the range of 21 to 25. The scripture says she was a widow for four score and four years. Anna was a widow for 84 years. What commitment. For 84 years, she embraced the mantle of abstinence and celibacy for the service of the Lord.

... And she was in the temple of God and serving the Lord in fasting and prayer.

1. She embraced this mantle, never losing the grace for fasting.
2. Fasting was her lifestyle, even as she increased in age.
3. Like her, we must see the significance of keeping the flesh under subjection.

Apostle Paul admonishes us, "Let's by any means, when I have preached to others that I become a castaway." Paul was another person who made himself a eunuch through the means of abstinence or celibacy for the sake of the kingdom. He too understood how necessary it was to put his flesh under subjection."

Father,

I thank you for allowing me to hear the word at your mouth. I could not have given them answers without hearing first from you. You summoned us to, "...Call upon You, promising to answer us and show us great and mighty things (Jeremiah 33:3)."

You allowed for the expounding and the exegesis of the text. You are Revelation! Thank you for the principal things. Thank you for understanding.

We loose grace upon all those you are calling to take the mantle and serve you in this capacity.

In Jesus' name, AMEN.

Made in the USA
Columbia, SC
11 July 2024

38252687R00107